HISTORY OF
MEHMED THE CONQUEROR

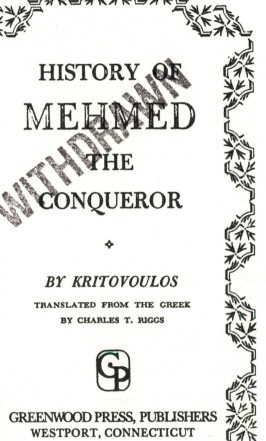

HISTORY OF
MEHMED
THE
CONQUEROR

✦

BY KRITOVOULOS

TRANSLATED FROM THE GREEK
BY CHARLES T. RIGGS

GREENWOOD PRESS, PUBLISHERS
WESTPORT, CONNECTICUT

Copyright 1954 by Princeton University Press

Reprinted by permission of Princeton University Press

Reprinted in 1970 by Greenwood Press
An imprint of Greenwood Publishing Group, Inc.
88 Post Road West, Westport, Connecticut 06881

Library of Congress Catalog Card Number 79-90541
ISBN 0-8371-3119-7

Printed in the United States of America

The paper used in this book complies with the
Permanent Paper Standard issued by the National
Information Standards Organization (Z39.48-1984).

10 9 8 7 6 5 4 3 2

PREFACE

STRANGE it is that the most vivid and accurate picture of a great series of campaigns should come from one of the defeated party—as if the great history of the American War of Independence had been written by an Englishman. But not only did a Greek write this story of the Turkish destruction of the Greek Empire, but it took another Greek to translate it into Turkish.

Equally strange is it that, while Kritovoulos distinctly states that he hopes to influence the Philhellenes in the British Isles by this story of a Turkish sultan, it has been necessary to wait nearly five hundred years before it is put in English.

The work of all authors, especially those who wrote five centuries ago, needs to be tested as to accuracy by the testimony of other contemporaries, and mature judgment on relative worth is not always easy. Everything known until the present, however, indicates that we have here a work of high value, written with the true genius of an historian and with commendable non-partisanship. When compared with the histories of such men as Phrantzes, Khalkondylis, and Dukas, the facts recorded by Kritovoulos seem to be more accurately given in general than the records of the others.

Very little can be found regarding the life and work of Kritovoulos, outside of this one work, which seems to have been his only one. He was a Greek, apparently a native of the island of Imbros in the north Aegean Sea. He was not present at the siege of Constantinople, which he describes so vividly; but very soon after its capture he visited the place and came into the service of the Conqueror, being finally appointed Governor of the island of Imbros. Apparently he became personally acquainted with Sultan Mehmed and studied his career most carefully. He admired the Sultan's military prowess and ability, even while mourning the loss of the City and the downfall of the last vestige of the Byzantine Empire. Modern Greek historians, such as Papparigopoulos, have been inclined to berate and undervalue Kritovoulos because he made a hero out of the man who defeated the Greeks. Yet such impartial judges as Professor Alexander Van Millingen of Robert College and Sir Edwin Pears, long the Doyen of the Constantinople Bar, rate Kritovoulos very high as an authority on matters pertaining to the entire campaign.

His history has been translated into French by Dr. Ph. A. Dethier and printed, but not published, at Budapest; it was also translated into Hungarian; and some thirty years ago it was at last published in a Turkish edition, translated by Carolides Efendi, Parliamentary Deputy for Smyrna. It now appears for the first time in English.

The work covers only the first seventeen years of the thirty-year reign of Mehmed II. Probably Kritovoulos intended to continue the history up to the end of that reign —as is indicated in several passages in the following pages (see Epistle, concluding paragraphs, and Part I, §6). It seems likely that his death prevented his accomplishing his purpose.

Marked peculiarities characterize this book: not only Kritovoulos' peculiar Byzantine phraseology but also his use of the ancient geographical names—calling the Albanians Illyrians, the Hungarians Paeonians, the Serbs the Triballi, the Danube River the Ister, the Black Sea the Euxine, etc., and giving Greek names for the provinces of Asia Minor. Especially noteworthy is the avoidance of the term, "Turks"; throughout his history Kritovoulos refers to the Ottomans as "Arabs and Persians."

One particular usage requires more elucidation: the name "Roman" is applied by Kritovoulos to the Greeks (Byzantines) of Constantinople, for, in common with most Easterners of the day, he regarded the City as New Rome and the Byzantine Empire as the Eastern Roman Empire—as it truly was in origin.

In the matter of proper names, Kritovoulos uses the Greek forms. Thus, he refers to the Sultan as Μεχεμέτης, which is

from the Turkish Mehmet, or Mehmed. The Sultan, sometimes referred to by scholars as Mohammed, is usually called
by the Turks Fatih Mehmed, or Mehmed the Conqueror,
which is the form used in this translation.

Kritovoulos also uses the Byzantine chronology, reckoning
5,508 years from the Creation to the birth of Christ, thus
making the year 1451, as the beginning of the reign of
Mehmed II, "6959 from the beginning."

The original manuscript of this valuable work is one of the
treasures of the Seraglio Point Museum Library in Istanbul
today, and it is carefully guarded as such. It was discovered
in the Library in 1865, and five years later was transcribed
by Herr Karl Müller and printed in Paris in *Fragmenta
Historicorum Graecorum*, Vol. V. The dedicatory Epistle to
Mehmed was published separately by Tischendorf in 1870.
The Paris edition of the history was unavailable to me, and I
have used the Hungarian edition.

The translator wishes to express his deep appreciation of
the stimulus and help rendered him, both in the undertaking
of this work and repeatedly as the work went on, by the
late lamented Dr. Walter Livingston Wright, Jr., whose encouragement and valuable suggestions contributed much to
whatever success it has.

The translator wishes also to express his deep obligation
and thanks to Professor Lewis V. Thomas, who, in the
midst of heavy responsibilities, has been willing to give time
and care to the reading of the manuscript and has made many
valuable emendations.

Robert College　　　　　　　　　　　　　　　　C.T.R.
Bebek, Istanbul, Turkey

HISTORY OF
MEHMED THE CONQUEROR

AN EPISTLE,

To the Supreme Emperor, setting forth the purpose of the book, and the events in brief which are therein recorded, and showing the reason for the composition.

To the Supreme Emperor, King of Kings, Mehmed, the fortunate, the victor, the winner of trophies, the triumphant, the invincible, Lord of land and sea, by the will of God, Kritovoulos the Islander, servant of thy servants.

SEEING that you are the author of many great deeds, O most mighty Emperor, and in the belief that the many great achievements of generals and kings of old, nor merely of Persians and Greeks, are not worthy to be compared in glory and bravery and martial valor with yours, I do not think it just that they and their deeds and accomplishments, as set forth in the Greek historians and their writings from contemporary times and up to the present, should be celebrated and admired by all, and that these should enjoy everlasting remembrance, while you, so great and powerful a man, possessing almost all the lands under the sun, and glorious in your great and brilliant exploits, should have no witness, for the future, of your valor and the greatest and best of your deeds, like one of the unknown and inglorious ones who are till now unworthy of any memorial or record in Greek; or that the deeds of others, petty as they are in comparison to yours, should be better known and more famed before men because done by Greeks and in Greek history, while your accomplishments, vast as they are, and in no way inferior to those of Alexander the Macedonian, or of the generals and kings of his rank, should not be set forth in Greek to the Greeks, nor passed on to posterity for the undying praise and glory of your deeds.

Indeed, you are the only one of kings, or at any rate one of a very few, who have united deeds with words and wisdom and majesty; for you are both a good king and a mighty warrior. So I have deemed it fitting and right, trusting in your favor, to undertake the present effort and commit to writing in Greek, as best I may, your merits and accomplishments, which far exceed in number and greatness those of any other.

Perhaps many of the honorable Arabs and Persians [Ottomans] may record these better and hand them on to our successors, for they know them well and have studied the facts; but nothing of this kind will take the place of a treatise in the Greek language, which has very great renown in all parts. For such writings will become known only among Arabs and Persians [Ottomans] and those who are familiar with their language. But these things will thus become the common pride and wonder, not of Greeks alone, but of all western nations, indeed those beyond the Pillars [of Hercules] and those who inhabit the British Isles, and many more, when they are translated into the language of those peoples who are Philhellenes and are learned in such matters. This also has roused me still more to this task, for I believe there will be many to judge and bear witness to my history.

Therefore, O mighty Emperor, I have already labored hard, for I was not myself a witness of the events, to know the exact truth about these things. In writing the history I have at the same time inquired of those who knew, and have examined carefully into how it all happened; and so I have composed this book in five divisions, beginning my story at the time when you commenced your reign, when first you crossed from Asia into Europe, as the successor of your father.

It contains also the war with the Romans [the Byzantines] and the capture of the City; the events in Enos, and against the Phoceans and the Triballi [the Serbs], as they occurred, and the complete defeat and enslavement of these peoples; further, the first and second invasion of the Peloponnesus by the Sultan, and how he subjugated it all and got possession of the cities therein, some by surrender, others by fighting, very strong as they were, and noteworthy—I refer to Corinth and Sparta and Tegea and Patras in Achaia. And he destroyed many strong fortresses, and compelled the whole of the Peloponnesus to pay tribute. Also his first expedition into Illyria [Albania], and his devastation of that land, and his further advance clear to its limits. Besides this, the campaign against Sinope and Trebizond, great and flourishing royal cities, and how he overcame them, as is well known, and conquered all their outlying territory.

Also, the revolt of Drakoulis, and the insurrection of the Getae [Wallachians], and the invasion of their land by the Sultan, and the overthrow and enslavement of both, and of how Rados was made ruler of them by the Sultan after the flight of his brother Drakoulis; and the capture of Mitylene and the whole of Lesbos, one of the greatest islands and one of the most famous and best known for its glory and size and power and riches; also the first and second expeditions into Dalmatia and against the Bostroi [Bosnians] and Paeonians [Hungarians], and how all the territory of these peoples was conquered and devastated; and of how he took fortified cities and fortresses, nearly three hundred of them, and their princes as well. Also the first and second expeditions against the Illyrians [Albanians] in the Ionic Gulf, and their destruction; and the five-years' war with the Venetians and their first and second defeats in the Peloponnesus by the governors, and how the Sultan quieted the feelings of these men.

Besides, it tells of the splendid and costly buildings he made in the city, of temples and arsenals and palaces and markets and porches and baths, also the walling and manning of very useful and necessary fortresses and colonies, both when he crossed the Hellespont and the Chersonese and when he crossed the Bosporus, and not a few other such things. And further, speeches of the greatest importance, of the times of the Sultan and of the people among whom these things occurred during seventeen years.

So, having written all these things and related them in this book, I now send it to your Royal attention and wisdom, to be examined and judged. And if the bravery recorded in it be in accord with the fact, and comparable to your acts, and it be attested by the Royal approval, I shall acknowledge my gratitude to God, and to you, O Sultan, for providing such material for me by the best of deeds for description by my words. And so I shall be encouraged to prepare for the coming effort, and joyfully give myself to the remaining part of the work which, under God, I shall undertake for you, simply trying to ascertain many of the imperatively needed facts now unknown to me—which is the reason for the delay until now of this whole manuscript.

And if my words seem far inferior to your deeds, so that they do not attain to the greatness of those acts—as indeed must be the case—let the book be condemned as useless, while I myself, reverencing you at a distance in silent awe, yield in the matter of historical record to others who in such things are far more competent than I.

The Castle of Rumeli Hisari built by Mehmed the Conqueror in 1452

PART I

S U M M A R Y

Including the beginning of the reign of the Great
Sultan Mehmed, his accession, his works and deeds,
the building of the new fortress on the Bosporus,
the battle for Constantinople and its capture.
Period included: three years [A.D. 1451-1453].*

* These brief summaries at the head of the five books are
written in the manuscript in purple ink by a different hand,
and are evidently not by the author himself.

Of the reasons for the composition

§ 1. Kritovoulos the Islander, originally of the inhabitants of Imbros, wrote this history in the belief that events so great and wonderful, occurring in our own times, should not remain unrecorded, but ought to be written up and handed down to subsequent generations so that brave deeds, well worth recording, certainly no less so than those of the old heroes, shall not disappear from the knowledge of men, being hidden by time. Thus those who live after us may not be greatly injured by being deprived of such a history and its lessons, and the authors of these deeds may have a fitting memorial for time to come of their heroism and valor, through this history and its portrait of these deeds.

§ 2. Hence it seemed to me, not the least for this reason, that this present history was needed. For ancient deeds, although very honored and very great, are somehow hard to accept as true, and it is with difficulty that they secure a hearing; as if, as time passes, they are credited or else despised in accordance with the general trend of memory. Everything redundant reaches the point of surfeit, and surfeit brings disgust. Whereas the modern, being new and near and well-known, is easily accepted and retained, and since it is nearby, it is the more admirable, still more so since it is more interesting and is credited because it is clear and well-known. Men for the most part prefer the more recent events and wish to study them rather than others.

§ 3. For these and similar reasons, the present history appears to me necessary. Great and remarkable deeds have been done here in our times, deeds such as were enacted in ancient times among both Greeks and barbarians, yea, deeds of valor like those of the most noteworthy men. A very great government, and the oldest we know, has been destroyed after a struggle of no long duration—that of the Romans [Byzantines]. And this has been the greatest event of all, and is a change in affairs that is of no little importance.

§ 4. I shall write of these things one by one, exactly as they occurred, suiting the words to the deeds, and never separating the deeds from the times when they took place, but preserving carefully the order as between persons and as between dates. And in all this I shall use the utmost care to tell the truth.

§ 5. The events previous to our times, what happened to this people in earlier days, what their sultans who followed one another in succession from those days till the present accomplished in the way of brave and remarkable deeds, the wars they waged, the victories they won, victories by which they gradually humbled the great rule of the Romans of former times and brought it to the point where they completely subdued and utterly destroyed it—all this has been narrated by many before me, and it is not my purpose now to record these things, nor is this the material for my present composition.

§ 6. Instead I shall write this out, God willing, in other books later on, devoting to it a separate treatise, setting forth accurately the dates, the events, and the grand achievements of that period.

§ 7. Even though many have told of these events, they have not done so systematically, nor have they arranged their history as should have been done, but have followed a sort of chance arrangement, either according to their own judgment, or else as they happened to remember it. They either lacked experience in writing history or else paid little attention to accuracy. However, my present composition does not treat of these things.

§ 8. My object is rather to present the deeds of the now reigning great Sultan Mehmed, excellent as they are and in every respect surpassing those of his predecessors. I give them as a result of my own study and from the accounts of my contemporaries, as a model and an excellent example to be followed by all who love bravery and courage. For this man excelled not only his own predecessors, but also the kings who were of his generation, in valor and courage, generalship and good fortune, and in his experience in military matters, as much as they excelled their predecessors and their contemporaries.

Apology

§ 9. So I beg of my compatriots, both those now living and those who in times to come may read this history, not to condemn me for either stupidity or perversity, if in place of grieving as others do over our misfortunes, or being burdened at the sufferings of our nation, I choose to record and to openly hold up to ridicule and disparagement our own internal evils, which—in others' views—ought rather to be covered up as far as possible and by no means brought to the notice of the public.

§ 10. First, then, let me say that I would not place any censure on my nation or proceed to slander or speak evil of my people. With a far different purpose have I embarked on the present effort. For I am not so past feeling or so bitter in my judgment as to wish to condemn the unfortunate rather than to share their pain. Nor would I criticize my race.

§ 11. Furthermore, I am not so stupid or so lacking in judgment, nor so altogether unacquainted with human affairs as not to recognize their fortunes and changes or the inconstancy, uncertainty, and irregularity of events, or to think that in such confusion and disorder of things, and in the diseases common to all mankind, I should seek in my own nation alone for healthy and stable and altogether immutable conditions, as though it were absolutely above all others and not under any circumstances to be compared or contrasted with any others.

§ 12. Who does not know that since men have existed the kingly or ruling power has not always remained in the same people, nor has it been limited to one race or nation? Like the planets, rule has gone from nation to nation and from place to place in succession, always changing and passing, now to the Assyrians, the Medes, the Persians, and then to the Greeks and Romans, according to the times and epochs establishing itself in a place and never returning to the same.

§ 13. There is therefore nothing astonishing if the same

11

things happen and are endured now also, and the Romans [Byzantines] lose their rule and prosperity, which pass on and are transferred to others, just as they came from others to them, so forever preserving the same nature and order of events. And since this is the case, how then can we possibly condemn our nation, with any justice, because it has not been able to preserve its happiness forever or to guard its supreme power and good fortune unshaken?

§ 14. And if certain individuals, who in their own times had the responsibility for affairs, have by the depravity of their character misdirected the affairs of empire and have not made proper use of circumstances, this is not a fault of the nation, but of those who have badly and wrongfully misused their opportunities. They alone should justly be held responsible, and the nation should not be condemned. In the same way the good should now be praised and their good deeds admired in every way and honored. We should not desire to deprive them of praise and of the rewards of virtue because of the indolence and wickedness of others, for this would not be just.

§ 15. This is what Josephus, the Hebrew, a truthful man well acquainted with the facts, recognizes in his book about the capture [of Jerusalem]. He praises the skill and valor of the Romans, and exalts them very truthfully in his discourse. He also reproaches the evils which appeared within his own nation, but he frees from blame those who had done no wrong. This is what I also shall try by all means to do, not shrinking in the least but preserving in every respect what is fitting and true. But enough of this; let us turn to our subject.

Beginning of the History

§ 16. It was the year 6959 from the beginning [A.D. 1451] when the Sultan Murad came to the end of his life, having lived a total of fifty-two years and having reigned thirty-one, a very good man in every way, high-minded, and also a very great general who had exhibited throughout his life many brave and wonderful deeds, as indeed these exploits show. He was the sixth of the brilliant line of the Ottomans, a nobleman of noblemen.

§ 17. These men are of the very oldest people, that of Achaemenes and Perses, and springing from them, all the kings of the Persians are descended. There were indeed Persians of other lines, as Herodotus relates, but they were common and ordinary while these were alone the illustrious line of kings—those who had their primitive origin from Achaemenes and Perses.

§ 18. So too the Greeks are descended from Danaus and Linges, who were in origin Egyptians, from the town of Chemis, situated in the marsh land. They migrated into Greece. Ages afterwards, the descendants of these people, who were called Achaemenidae and Persidae, crossed over into Asia and settled at first in Persia. And when they died, they left their race and name to that place.

§ 19. So when this Murad, of whom I spoke, died, his son Mehmed succeeded to the sultanate, he being the seventh Sultan and now in the twentieth year of his life. He was sent for from Asia, for it was there that he had his province which had been assigned him by his father.

§ 20. Just at that period the Divine power sent many unusual, unexpected, and prodigious signs. These occurred both at the birth of this man and also at his entering on his rule as Sultan. For strange and exceptional earthquakes took place, and subterranean rumblings, also severe thunder and lightning from heaven, and whirlwinds and terrible storms, and an unusual light appeared in the sky, and many similar signs which the Divine power is accustomed to exhibit at the time of the greatest events and changes in the customary order.

§ 21. The soothsayers, sages and prophets and inspired persons foretold and foresaw many things that were to happen, and announced that the new Sultan would have every sort of good fortune and virtue, that his dominion would be very large in every way, and that he would surpass all the sultans before him in the very great abundance of his glory and wealth and power and accomplishments.

§ 22. When he became heir to a great realm and master

of many soldiers and enlisted men, and had under his power already the largest and best parts of both Asia and Europe, he did not believe that these were enough for him nor was he content with what he had: instead he immediately overran the whole world in his calculations and resolved to rule it in emulation of the Alexanders and Pompeys and Caesars and kings and generals of their sort.

How the Sultan was also a Philosopher

§ 23. His physical powers helped him well. His energies were keen for everything, and the power of his spirit gave him ability to rule and to be kingly. To this end also his wisdom aided, as well as his fine knowledge of all the doings of the ancients. For he studied all the writings of the Arabs and Persians [Ottomans], and whatever works of the Greeks had been translated into the language of the Arabs and Persians—I refer particularly to the works of the Peripatetics and Stoics. So he used the most important philosophies of the teachers of the Arabs and Persians.

Treaties of the Sultan with Constantine, King of the Romans [Byzantines], and Karaman

§ 24. He did not postpone anything or put off any action, but immediately carried everything through. First he made a treaty with the Romans and the Emperor Constantine [XIII];[1] and after that, with Karaman,[2] the ruler of Upper Phrygia and Cilicia, believing that for the present this move was beneficial to his affairs.

Scrutiny of the lists of the army, etc.

§ 25. Then he gave himself to an examination of his whole realm. Using his judgment about the governorships of the nations under him, he deposed some of the governors and substituted others who he deemed to be superior to the former in strategy and knowledge and justice. It was his aim,

[1] Constantine XIII Palaeologus, 1448-1453.
[2] The most important of the Anatolian Seljuks' successor-states, and the Ottomans' principal Anatolian Moslem rival.

above all, to have every province under him ruled as well and as justly as possible.

§ 26. He also went over the registers and battle order of the troops, cavalry and infantry, which are paid from the royal treasuries. He especially made the royal palace subject of considerable thought and increased the pay of its troops. I refer to the "new recruits," his personal guard of foot-soldiers, customarily called in their own language Yenitsari [Janissaries], a term meaning "new levy." He realized how important these were for himself, for the protection of his person and of the whole realm.

§ 27. In addition to this, he collected a supply of arms and arrows and other things needful and useful in preparation for war. Then he examined his family treasury, looking especially closely into its overseers. He carefully questioned the officials in charge of the annual taxes and obliged them to render accounts.

Examination of the Public Funds, and of their Treasurers

§ 28. And he discovered that much of the public and royal revenue was being badly spent and wasted to no good purpose, about one-third of the yearly revenues which were recovered for the royal treasury. So he set the keeping of this in good order. He greatly increased the annual revenue. He brought many of the tax officials to reason through fear, and for them substituted trustworthy and wise men to collect and safe-keep the funds. His father had dealt with such matters in a much more hit-or-miss manner, but he made short work of them.

§ 29. So, with the arrangement of these affairs in this fashion, the ordering of the reign in the best possible manner, there passed the year 6959 from the beginning [A.D. 1451], the first year of the reign of the Sultan. Thus he prepared for greater things; and so everything contributed to the plan he had before him.

§ 30. And this plan was: he meant to build a strong fortress on the Bosporus on the European side, opposite to the

Asiatic fortress on the other side, at the point where it is narrowest and swiftest, and so to control the straits by uniting both continents, Asia and Europe; and to cross there whenever he should choose, quite independently of any other individuals and with no least question that it was the Sultan himself who controlled the passage.

§ 31. For he well knew how many and what varied difficulties this problem had presented to those of previous times, in the days of his forefathers, and especially of his father—what a hindrance this had offered to their operations, and how it had frequently almost made them abandon the other continent. Meanwhile the Emperor of the Romans [Byzantines] reigned securely in the City, always watching the times and the events, for the most part controlling the sea, making use of it sometimes to the advantage of his own nation, and injuring whom he pleased. In addition, the Italians, and especially the Venetians, in their quarrels with these others, often cruised in long triremes through the Bosporus and the Hellespont, preventing the crossing of these straits.

§ 32. Not only did these facts influence him, but, in looking toward his set purpose, he also believed it would be wise to have a walled fortress. And in connection with the siege of the City, which he planned for the not distant future, he believed that a very strong fortification would shut off from the City not only the two continents of Asia and Europe, but also both seas, from above, the Euxine Sea through the Bosporus, and from below, the Aegean and all the Grecian sea through the Hellespont.

§ 33. With this plan in mind, that winter he ordered all the materials to be prepared for building, namely, stone and timbers and iron and whatever else would be of use for this purpose. He set the best and most experienced officers over the work, instructing them to put everything speedily in the best order, so that when spring came he could undertake the task.

§ 34. The Emperor Constantine, on the other hand, and the men of the City, when they learned this, regarded it as terrible and as the beginning of great evils. Considering it a certain danger of enslavement—as indeed it was—they de-

16

cided to fortify their town and to prepare the whole City.
They were sorely troubled.

§ 35. Hence he [Constantine] decided to send an embassy
composed of his associates to try by any possible means
to forestall this threat.

§ 36. And they, when they arrived, used all sorts of arguments, citing the treaties and agreements. They told how, in
all the previous treaties which had been drawn up and ratified,
both with his forefathers and with his father, and indeed
with him also, it was in every case promised that no one
should build a fortress or anything else in this place. Furthermore it was specified that, if any such undertaking was begun, both sides would oppose this by every possible means.
So the country had been saved from danger of this until now
and was free. They said they would agree simply to the passing across of the Sultan's armies and other equipment from
continent to continent, but they demanded that he should not
in any way break the treaties, concluded but yesterday and
the day before, for any trivial reason. For surely he did not
wish to commit any injustice, as they certainly were not doing any injustice on their part.

Reply of Sultan Mehmed to the Ambassadors

§ 37. The Sultan replied to them: "I have no intention
to do you any injustice, O Romans, nor to do anything contrary to the agreements and treaties in this undertaking of
mine, but only to protect my possessions while doing no injury to you. It is, however, just and right for each of us to
guard and make sure of his own, not in the least injuring
those with whom he has a treaty, and this is the desire of
all. But, as you see, I rule over both Asia and Europe, continents separated from each other, and in each of these I have
many opponents and enemies of my rule. I am obliged to be
present everywhere and to be equal to the needs of both continents if I do not wish to be taken by surprise—which is what
my enemies wish. And know this well, that the Italian
triremes gave us many great difficulties in the days of my
father when we wished to cross against the Paeonians [Hun-

garians] who were attacking us—how they sailed and prevented us from crossing. We must therefore stop this threat from them and make our sea safe and not suffer the injury, and still more the shame, cast on us by everyone, that we cannot guard our own seas and dominions. Besides, this place where I am now going to build a fortress is our own, being the place for crossing into our own territory, whether from Asia into Europe or from Europe into Asia. So you must not interfere too much. If you wish to enjoy peace, and if you have no intention on your part of preventing us from having this crossing-place, I on my part will neither break my pledges nor desire to do so, provided you will stay in your own place and not meddle at all in our affairs nor wish to be too prying."

§ 38. With this reply, he dismissed the ambassadors. They on their return told everything to the Emperor Constantine and all the Romans [Byzantines]—the whole story and especially that it was not possible to prevent this undertaking entirely, either by argument or by persuasion, but only by resort to force, if indeed that were possible. And they, since they fully realized the exceeding gravity of the situation and that there was nothing they could do, kept an unwilling silence.

Activity of the Sultan by land and sea, and his arrival at the Bosporus for the fortification of the castle

§ 39. Sultan Mehmed, at the very first opening of spring, as everything had been prepared for him, filled thirty triremes and armed them fully as for a naval fight—in case that should be necessary, or if there were any resistance. He prepared other ships to carry the equipment, and sent them up from Gallipoli to the Bosporus.

§ 40. He himself with a large army went by land. On arrival at the straits on the seventh day, he halted his army; and taking with him some of the strongest young men and also some of the older men whom he knew as having intimate knowledge of the surroundings, he himself reconnoitered on

18

horseback to spy out the country and its topography, especially with the greatest care the narrow part at the crossing, exceedingly narrow, with its twisting curves, densely wooded promontories, retreating bays and bends.

§ 41. At the swiftest point of the current, with its resulting whirlpools and eddies made by the promontories and everything else making the crossing most perplexing and difficult, he established his ferry.

§ 42. The ancient Greeks, knowing these facts, called the district "Symplegades."[3] They said Hercules was the first man to pass here, and after him was Jason with his Argonauts. They had the greatest difficulty, because they were shut in on every side and hemmed in and tangled up by the narrowness of the passages and of the channel and the frequent recesses and the jutting out of the promontories, so that it seemed as if the land were on all sides of them as they sailed up or down, and they felt as though confined in the middle of a small lake with no outlet.

§ 43. On account of the great noise and swift current of these waters, borne down from the Euxine Sea, that very great and extensive sea to the north which comes down and ends in a very narrow part, great waves are raised by the rush and force of the current as it bubbles and swirls and drives boats along, dashing them against the rocks and sinking them unless indeed great care and skill are exercised by the sailors in them. On measuring the width of the strait to find the narrowest point, he found it to be about seven stadia.[4]

§ 44. After examining and considering all these matters and deciding only after most careful thought, the Sultan came to the conclusion that this was the most suitable place, and made up his mind to build the castle there. He marked out with stakes the location where he wished to build, planning the position and the size of the castle, the foundations, the distance between the main towers and the smaller turrets, also the bastions and breastworks and gates, and every other detail as he had carefully worked it out in his mind. He then

[3] The Symplegades were small islands in the Black Sea entrance to the Bosporus and had no connection with the narrows where Sultan Mehmed constructed his castle.

[4] The actual distance is ca. 1,800 feet.

portioned it out in detail, ordering his men to undertake the work with the utmost speed, and offering prizes of a splendid character to those who should accomplish it best and most speedily.

He builds the walls and the castle in the strongest way

§ 45. And he himself undertook the portion of the castle along by the sea, and began the work of building in the middle of the spring, with a large force of men and at great expense. And through the zeal and rivalry of all who were employed on the work, before the summer had entirely passed, he had walled the castle, the best fortified, safest, and most renowned of all castles ever built. He worked it out with very large stones, carefully selected and fitted together. The joints were strengthened with much iron and lead and many other things, and it was fortified and made secure by the great massive towers, solidly constructed and raised to a great height, and by the strength of the smaller towers and bastions plus the height and thickness of the wall.

The Plan of the Castle

§ 46. The thickest part of the wall was twelve cubits wide. Its height was four times that, and the size of the fortress was not like a castle, but rather like a small town. He made the shape of the castle triangular. The sides of the right angle went up the ascent to the summit, for the locality had a gradual slope, each like an outwork with its tower projecting, very strong and very large, uniting the two transverse sides and guarding them.

§ 47. And the two corners of the base, along the shore, on each end of the side thus walled in, were strengthened by other towers; these were smaller in size than the ones at the apexes, but by no means deficient in strength.

§ 48. He planned this form and this place for the castle, in the first place so that he might control as much of the shore as possible, for the sake of the stone-hurling machines. The thicker parts of the wall were toward the sea, so that the machines might close the straits and sink the ships. In the second place, by holding the points at the top and guarding them, he might keep the warriors of the enemy as far away as possible, so that they might not shoot down from above on those manning the battlements and wound them but would have to keep at a respectful distance.

The Place of the Stone-Throwing Machines

§ 49. After building the fortification in the aforementioned manner, he prepared all sorts of weapons: javelins and bows and spears, also helmets and shields and many more such arms. And in addition to these, with cannon and larger or smaller crossbows he armed all the battlements of the great towers and the smaller towers and bastions.

§ 50. And the largest of the cannon he placed by the seashore, on the ground under the wall, putting them close together along the whole side, pointing at the sea, as I said. They were not all in a straight line, but pointed in various directions at the deep water and guarded both directions, those on the right facing left, and those on the left facing right and firing from the right, thus cutting off the passage of the straits. For they hurled immense round stones that went along the surface of the sea as if they were swimming.

How the Uniting of the Continents was Done

§ 51. From this castle toward the one opposite, and again from that one to this in the same way, other cannon prevented the passing through, not only of galleons or triremes, but of any freight boat or small cargo ship and even of the smallest boat, on penalty of being sunk or broken to bits and being condemned to be sent to the bottom. And this by night as well as by day, unless a ship passed by the consent of the commander of the castle.

§ 52. Thus the management of the castle was arranged for by him, and in this way he united the two continents and placed the crossing under his own control. So then, having fortified it well and armed it, and made it impregnable to all, or in other words absolutely immune to capture, and having left there a sufficient garrison, and having appointed one of his most trustworthy men as commander of the castle, and put in charge of the cannon men who could use them skilfully and well, he went back to Adrianople, since the autumn was already waning. And so the 6960th year from the beginning passed by, which was the second of the Sultan's reign [A.D. 1452].

Return of the Sultan to Adrianople and the Building of the New Palace

§ 53. During the same period he also built a splendid palace near Adrianople, on the banks of the Hebrus River beyond the city. It was adorned with splendid stones and transparent marbles, and was resplendent with much gold and silver within and without and embellished with sculptures and paintings and with many other costly things carefully designed and wrought. Around it he planted gardens decked with all sorts of shrubs and domestic trees bearing beautiful fruit. In these gardens he put various kinds of domestic and wild animals and flocks of birds, and made the place attractive with many other beautiful things which he knew would bring enjoyment and beauty and pleasure. And in his zeal he constructed a royal courtyard very near this, and made ample barracks for the new cavalry and infantry troops, in it and around it, guarding the palace on all sides.

§ 54. He also resolved to carry into execution immediately the plan which he had long since studied out and elaborated in his mind and toward which he had bent every purpose from the start, and to wait no longer nor delay. This plan was to make war against the Romans [Byzantines] and their Emperor Constantine and to besiege the city. For he thought, as was true, that if he could succeed in capturing it and becoming master of it, there was nothing to hinder him from sallying forth from it in a short time, as from a stronghold for all the environs, and overrunning all and subduing them to himself. For this reason he could no longer be restrained at all. He did not think he ought to stay quiet in his own

22

parts any longer and maintain peace, but believed he should speedily make war and capture the city.

§ 55. There were also certain supernatural signs that urged him to this, together with some oracles, auguries, soothsayings, and other such things, to which he gave great weight, and on which men rely to tell them the future. All these pointed to the same conclusion, and gave him strong hopes that he could capture the city. So, calling together all those in authority, that is, the governors, the generals, the captains of cavalry, the majors of battalions, and the chiefs of the soldiery, he made them the following address.

Speech of the Sultan inciting his followers to battle against the city. Also a recital of previous deeds of his forefathers, and a brief survey of the entire rule

§ 56. "My friends and men of my empire! You all know very well that our forefathers secured this kingdom that we now hold at the cost of many struggles and very great dangers and that, having passed it along in succession from their fathers, from father to son, they handed it down to me. For some of the oldest of you were sharers in many of the exploits carried through by them—those at least of you who are of maturer years—and the younger of you have heard of these deeds from your fathers. They are not such very ancient events nor of such a sort as to be forgotten through the lapse of time. Still the eyewitness of those who have seen testifies better than does the hearing of deeds that happened but yesterday or the day before.

Of the Courage of the Heroes

§ 57. "It is perfectly possible to see even now, all over our land, signs of those deeds clearly shown—the walls of castles and towns torn down but yesterday or the day before, the ground, so to speak, still red and damp with their blood, and many other such clearly-read monuments of their heroism and valor stand as ever-memorable proofs of their courage in danger. And they exhibited in it all such heroism of spirit and firmness of purpose, and greatness of mind that, from

23

the very beginning, from their very small kingdom and power, they set their minds on the destruction of the rule of the Romans [Byzantines], and hoped to secure complete power over Asia and Europe.

Of the Conquest of Asia

§ 58. "And indeed, they did not belie themselves. Sallying forth at the start from the mountains of Cilicia and Taurus, with a small force, as I said, but with the greatest forethought and prudence, they quickly overran Lycia, Pamphylia, and upper Phrygia. They destroyed the Lydians, Carians, Mysians, and lower Phrygians and the Ionians, all of the Greek seacoast. Then they subdued the Galatians, Cappadocians, Pamphlagonians, Chalybians, Bithynians, Hellespontians—in a word, all the land which the Taurus encloses from Cilicia clear to Sinope on the Euxine Sea, which territory they call Lower Asia, they captured within a short time and made it secure for themselves.

The Beginning of the Crossing into Europe

§ 59. "They made themselves masters of all this region and of its coasts, and gained a firm control over the cities in it. And having established their capital in Brusa, they crossed the Hellespont in fairly great numbers, it is true, but not for open warfare, rather for plundering and quick surprise raids as opportunity offered. At the same time they were held in check by the sea, because the Romans [Byzantines] had control of it. But they captured the peak of the mountain in front of the monument of Helle, opposite the isthmus of Chersonesus, and having taken the castle there, by assault or by stratagem, they at first made raids from there and used the methods of banditry and of unforeseen attack and plunder, despoiling those who were near by.

The Conquest of Europe

§ 60. "But when they had advanced a short distance and were constantly becoming numerically stronger, they also captured some of the near-by fortresses, some by force of assault and others through stratagems. Thus they came down into the plain, and there nothing was any obstacle to them any more. They occupied the level country, sacked the villages and captured the cities, overthrew castles, defeated armies, and subdued many peoples. In a word, they overran without much delay the whole of Thrace and Macedonia. So they destroyed the Mysians [Bulgarians], who lived in the interior and along the Ister [Danube] River; also the Illyrians [Albanians], the Triballians [Serbs], the Hellenes, and many other races, and they subdued mighty castles and many large cities, some of them inland and others lying along the coasts.

§ 61. "But why should I waste time enumerating cities and nations? All the land that the Danube bounds, from its mouths at the Euxine Sea up to the junction with the Save, and going thence inland between the Bistres [Bosnians] and the Dalmatians between the Save and the Albanians, toward the south and west as far as the Ionian Gulf [the Adriatic Sea]—all this they conquered and overthrew, subjecting to taxation all who were in it. In addition, they conquered the Getae [Wallachians] beyond the Danube, and not only that, but all the coastlands except the Peloponnesus, a territory with a circumference of more than a thousand stadia.

§ 62. "All this was not done without toil, nor as if one did it by simply speaking the word, nor without opposition and resistance by those who were strong enough to resist. Nor did they get the mastery without bloodshed and without dangers. And they have not kept it till now without these. It cost them much blood, many wounds, and much sweat and pain.

§ 63. "For many great nations in both Asia and Europe took up arms against them, and struggled bravely, even to death, in behalf of liberty, and with valor. And many large cities among these peoples, fortified by walls and the bodies and arms and wealth and valor of their inhabitants, and many other things, rose up to resist. And fortified castles that were hard to capture, and places hard to cross, and many difficulties, and numerous rivers not easily crossed, and many such obstacles delayed them.

In Praise of Those Men and Their Kings

§ 64. "But the greatest obstacle of all was the forces of the Romans [Byzantines], both on land and on sea, always opposing them and fighting them and giving them much resistance and many struggles. Still, none of these things checked their forward progress, or curbed their impetuosity and valor until, having overthrown and completely demolished all, they firmly held the rule. They showed everyone their great strength, being valorous men to the very end and never yielding anything, from the very start, of their plans and ideals. Whenever they conquered their enemies, they went forward against them a great distance. And when they were beaten, they did not fall back or give up their good hope, but because of their confidence in themselves and their hope for the future, they endured everything, even when it was unknown to the Fates; moreover they bore up valiantly under events, daring even beyond their powers, taking unbelievable risks, and keeping good hope even in the worst circumstances.

§ 65. "They were also unyielding in distress, indefatigable in whatever they thought was advantageous to them, and eager for none of the pleasant things. They were quick to recognize duty, and swift to put into execution what they conceived as such. They always took delight in long absences from home in order to get possession of something they did not have. They were never content with what they had, nor did they allow others to be. They did not consider what was present as of any value, for they always went after the things they did not have, and they considered what they had not yet attained but which they had in mind, as if they already had it. They got very little encouragement out of what they already had, because of their desire for greater things, even though they toiled hard to gain and enjoy what they did not have. Their bodies they used as though they belonged to other persons as far as pain or danger was concerned. They did not in the least spare them, often even for mistaken purposes, and they kept their spirits unconquered. Thus, laboring all through their epoch, they chose for themselves a life full of struggles and pains. So they brought the realm

26

to such a point of glory and strength, by their numbers and wealth and by the arms and ships and all that they had, and handed it down to us very great in appearance and most capable for either war or peace. Let us not seem to betray the trust!

§ 66. "Our part, then, is not to destroy the achievements of our ancestors, nor detract from our own glory which we have secured through a long period. We are famed among all peoples for our courage and strategy and valor, and until now have been considered, and rightly so, as unconquerable. But now we are defeated by one city, and that one no longer daring to trust to itself but almost emptied of all its inhabitants and entirely cut off from and deprived of all the good things it previously enjoyed by the long-continued and repeated attacks and sieges of our forces, so that it is no longer a city but survives only in name. As for the rest, it is only farm land and an enclosure of plants and vineyards, as you see, and worthless houses and empty walls, most of them in ruins. And you see how it is located in the midst of our realm, finely situated by land and sea, how many great difficulties it has given us from the beginning, and still gives us now—always fighting against us, lying in wait for our goods and battening on our misfortunes and injuring us as much as possible.

The Crossing of the Ister [Danube] by the Paeonians [Hungarians] and Their Defeat by Beyazid

§ 67. "For who does not know how, in the days of our forefather Beyazid, their king roused the whole west against us, from the ocean and Marseilles, and the western Gauls, the inhabitants of the Pyrenees and of Spain, from the Rhine river and those of the extreme north, the Celts and the Celtiberians and the Germans, the king of the Paeonians and the Dacians.[5] The latter sent a great force of soldiers by land and also triremes down the river, and these, crossing the Ister [Danube] and coming down the banks of that

---

[5] Sigismund of Hungary, leader of the "Crusade" of Nicopolis (1396).

river, encamped in our territory. Nor did they have any less object in view than to destroy all our power and rule and to drive us out of both Europe and Asia, had it not been for the expedition of Beyazid at that time. His experience and daring prevented this, dispersed them, and completely conquered and annihilated them, so that some were cut to pieces, others were drowned in the Danube, while of the immense number only a few escaped, and were barely saved.

§ 68. "And again, shortly after, when she [the city of Constantinople] had stirred up Timur the Scythian [Tamerlane the Great] from Babylon against us, and urged him on, we suffered under him, as you know. And at that time we came within a very little of losing all our rule and power, that is, of losing one of the continents. From that time up to the present, the city has unceasingly and constantly plotted against us, armed our own people against each other, created disorders, and disturbed and injured our realm.

§ 69. "Yesterday and a short time ago she stirred up John the Goth,[6] with the Paeonians and Dacians against us. He crossed the Danube River two or three times with his army, and invaded our land and did much against my father. I pass over all the things we have suffered because of deserters, and the injury and loss this causes, which have occurred to us every day, for the words not only of slaves but also of free men should be brief. The city has not ceased, nor will it ever cease, withstanding and resisting our forces. Nor will it give up warring against us and stirring up trouble, as long as we allow it to remain in their possession. We must entirely destroy it, or else be enslaved under their hand.

§ 70. "So then, my friends, since such a city as this has set itself against us and does all it can against us, both openly and in secret, and plots against our power, should we hesitate and do nothing? Shall we not hasten to destroy it ere it does us great damage? Do we think it will always be in our power to arrange for battle where we like? And do we not know that we should not wait for wars and crises to come upon us, that we should never despair of gaining an opportunity, that

6 John Hunyadi.

the affairs of Fate are everywhere uncertain and the outcome of things is undetermined and unproved?

§ 71. 'Thinking men should always take time by the forelock and attack their enemies while they have the opportunity, and not wait till they suffer evils before defending themselves, but rather act before they suffer and take measures against the enemy beforehand rather than afterwards. One should in such cases consider as a gain whatever precautions one can take in deceiving or in forcing the enemy. For the fortunes of war do not go by schedule, but victory comes in most cases to him who can conceal his moves or anticipate the foe, and so gain something above what he already has.

§ 72. "My men, since I am of this opinion and have reasoned out the thing and have these motives, and further since I am so stirred by these great crimes, I have gathered you together here, for I consider the situation no longer tolerable. I recognize the right of all who are so persuaded to make known their opinion to me. And I maintain that we must undertake this, and fight quickly, and must accept war and capture the City with all determination and speed, or never lay claim to our realm any more, or to its possessions as our own, or think of anything as certain for the future. For our own realm cannot be free of fear, or our goods out of danger, unless this City be either captured or destroyed by us.

§ 73. "The matter is very simple: I prefer either to hold our empire with this City also, or without it to be bereft of our empire as well. For if we get the City, you may be sure that our possessions will be secure and what we do not now have may also be secured. But without it, or while it is as at present, nothing we have is safe, and we can hope for nothing additional. If these people hold the City and are hard pressed by us, they will secure some stronger alliance and will hold the seas that are rightfully ours, and we shall be constantly at war and in danger and put to ruinous expenses, and the result of the war will be uncertain.

§ 74. "War is always likely to bring in such a case many illogical and unexpected results, and the prolongation of war subjects many things to chance. Again, if unable to save the

29

City, they should turn it over to others stronger than themselves and better equipped in men, money, ships, arms, and everything, and these should oppose our plans still more vigorously and withstand us as if in defense of their own homes—think what would then be our condition! A city so large, situated so favorably by land and sea and forever attacking our forces and taking advantage of our weak points and getting a preponderating power, would fight with us on equal terms. I myself believe—but I do not wish to say anything distressing! May such blasphemy be turned against the heads of our enemies! Even if it is terrible to hear, such things are not for us or for our good.

§ 75. "Wherefore we must no longer delay, or let slip the opportunity we have, but must attack the City, all of us, with all our men and power. Especially now that the Divinity is with us, we must not spare anything needed for the war, either men, or money, or arms, or anything else of that sort, and we must not consider anything else as more important until we have by every means captured it, or entirely destroyed it, or have been brought under subjection to them.

§ 76. "Let none of you think the City cannot be taken, or reason from the experience of my grandfather and my father, who, being of my opinion from the very beginning, carried on merciless warfare against it with a surpassingly large force of men and power, and arms, and made use also of a long siege and terrible famine, but were nevertheless still unable to conquer it.

§ 77. "If it had then withstood by its own strength and power, and had showed itself better than its attackers in troops and funds and arms and everything else, and had been better protected, or if they of our side had been unsuccessful because they were weaker in their own forces and preparations and so were never able to capture it, then this line of reasoning would be correct.

§ 78. "But who does not know that an unexpected piece of luck, coming in contrary to all logic, snatched victory out of the hands of Beyazid—a thing that often happens to man from the Divinity. For an agreement had been reached that the people of the City should surrender the City and themselves on a certain day, since they were unable to resist any longer on account of the famine due to the long siege. Then suddenly there appeared from Europe the king of the Paeonians and Dacians, and shortly thereafter, from Asia, Timur the Babylonian, and they made him raise the siege and turned him off to attack them. That was how this came about: the City was saved by an unexpected piece of good fortune.

§ 79. "You know also with what preparation and with what a large force my father set out against it, and how he had succeeded so well with the siege of the City that not even the wall itself could protect the defenders, who were hit by the archers and by the stones hurled by the machines. Indeed he had the City in his hands and would have captured it by the force of his weapons, had not those who were extremely near of kin to him, and whom he especially trusted, worked secretly against him and, what is particularly inexplicable, had they not taken the part of the besieged for the sake of their own gain. Thus, then, they made him give up the siege, and saved the City.

§ 80. "But even if at that time this had resulted from the strength of the Greeks themselves—for we even make this supposition!—still, the circumstances then and now are not the same, for the City or for us. For at that time the City had the benefit of wiser and more warlike persons and of those more experienced in affairs. It was guarded by the Emperor and his officers and by more inhabitants than now, and it had authority over that part of the sea next to the City. It also had at that time some assistance from the Italians and was hopeful of more, and it had many other sorts of help.

§ 81. "But now, things are weaker for the City, and in everything it is worse off. It has been to a great extent emptied of inhabitants, and is wholly cut off by sea. And its Emperor and his entourage are exactly the sort one might wish to have as adversaries. As for help from the Italians, they have hardly even a hope of this. Nay, rather they are actually fighting as enemies over their differing religious beliefs, and their internal organization is full of sedition and disturbance on this very account. And by carefully examining other points, one would find many other deficiencies.

31

§ 82. "As for us, our powers have grown very much by proficiency along many lines. We have enrolled soldiers, both horse and foot, more and better and better equipped than ever, and our youth are much more manly. Our royal court now enjoys its greatest power. We have the greatest wealth and a very great supply of treasure and of annual tribute and of arms and of machines and other implements for war, and not a few triremes plus many other things. All this would enable us to fight, not only against this one city but against many cities, even if we had to divide our forces and attack them all.

§ 83. "Furthermore we hold the sea, both on our own shores and also along all theirs. We have fortified it above and below the City, along both straits, with castles, shutting off the City from both continents by land and by sea. And we have not a few other advantages, because of which I hope, nay, am practically certain, that it will not be able to resist at all, but we shall either capture it by attack through the power of our arms, or take it after a brief siege.

§ 84. "Only, let us not delay, nor give the City time any longer to plot against us, but let us show ourselves brave men as soon as possible and prove to them and to all men that the City has survived until now, not because we lack valor, or because of our cowardice or weakness, carelessness and softness. Let us not shame the valor and virtues of our forefathers, nor appear unworthy of them by allowing one city in the midst of our empire—and such an empire!—to act as a tyrant and in every way to plot against us. Rather let us show ourselves to be of their line, sharing in their manliness and valor.

§ 85. "For they overran in a short time all of Asia and Europe and conquered them by their own efforts and perils. They captured many great cities, stormed fortified castles, and became masters of countless peoples. And we shall capture this City. Then, sallying forth from it as from an acropolis, with little trouble we shall overrun all the rest in a little while, and nothing shall be able to stand before us nor shall a single one of the rest be able to resist our power and rule, but in a short time we shall be masters of land and sea.

§ 86. "Let us not then delay any longer, but let us attack the City swiftly with all our powers and with this conviction: that we shall either capture it with one blow or shall never withdraw from it, even if we must die, until we become masters of it.

§ 87. "And I myself will first of all be with you and gladly share your travails, and will direct everything in the best way. I will reward the brave with appropriate gifts, each after his worth and valor, according as each is conspicuous in danger or distinguished for some special exploit."

Voting for War by the Sultan and by All

§ 88. So, when he had said this, he cast his vote for war. And practically all of those present applauded what was said by the Sultan, praising him for his good will and knowledge, bravery and valor, and agreeing with him, and still further inciting each other to war—some of them because of their own ambition and hope of gain, hoping from that time on to make something out of it and secure more riches for themselves, others to please the Sultan and at the same time wishing to make some gain themselves out of such affairs, and still others, with no knowledge of war—those who were young and inexperienced in such things.

§ 89. But those whose ideas were against the step for various reasons and especially because of the misfortunes they had had in war and the difficulties usually attendant on it, wanted to advise against making war. However, seeing the insistence and zeal of the Sultan, they were afraid, as it seems to me, and unwillingly yielded and were carried along with the majority. So the war was sanctioned by all.

Attack and Pillage of those outside the City

§ 90. So he immediately ordered the governor of Europe to raise an army quickly and attack the City itself and the region around it, and whatever other regions belonged to the Romans. This man immediately without delay raised an army, attacked everything around the City, and went up to the very gates of the City, plundering. He also attacked

33

Selymbria and its environs, and he disarmed the seacoasts near it, Perinthus also, and other places. Then the fortress of the Epibatae surrendered to him of its own accord. He dismantled also the region of the Black Sea, as much as was subject to the Romans, and he captured the fortress in Mesimbria also, which surrendered of its own accord. And the rest he plundered and did with them as he pleased.

§ 91. The Emperor Constantine and the men of the City, amazed at the speed of the movement and the unexpected attack and seeing hopelessly this unproclaimed war coming upon them—for it was but a short time since they had made a treaty with the attackers—despaired utterly of any further negotiations on these matters or of appealing to the agreements for peace. They were sure that this was impossible, for they saw the impetuosity of the Sultan to achieve his end, and all that had been so quickly done by him from the start, and how all those things came to no good purpose. Hence they expected a siege such as the City had never experienced before and a merciless war on land and sea, and all the evils of war: capture, and the sufferings of captivity, the killing of young and old, the plunder of their goods, the defiling of temples, and the enslaving and outrage of women and children.

§ 92. They did not believe they could resist, even for a short time, since they were faced with so great a war by land and sea. Therefore their morale was poor from the very beginning and they were in utter despair and could think of no useful move to meet the situation. They gave themselves up in their thoughts to something hopeless and unthinkable, and resigned themselves readily, with no longer any hope of safety.

§ 93. And they had good reason to do so. For in previous sieges they had had many things in their favor, and had had great hopes of surviving. They then had control over the neighboring seas and had to fight only on land. And this they could easily manage, for they faced the foe simply on one side—the land side—while on both seas they could sail with their galleons and transports. Further, their commerce then brought them great abundance of necessary supplies and other things. The City also was then full of both foreigners and citizens. They had much money stored up, both in public funds and in private and sacred funds, and also arms, ships, javelins, and all sorts of other things were abundantly prepared for the City, so that the siege scarcely seemed to be a siege.

§ 94. But now everything seemed and actually was the very opposite. The sea was cut off at both upper and lower straits by fortresses, and navigation was utterly impossible. Both continents were the scene of fighting, and a large fleet was expected which would make an attack on the sea-walls. It seemed altogether impossible that they would have enough soldiers for the whole circuit of the City, because of the lack of men. Further, it came at a time of great scarcity of money, both public and private, and the City suffered from the want of all sorts of things. And they saw no help for them from any direction.

§ 95. What disturbed them no less were the inexplicable events happening just then, events which they took as divine portents—unusual and strange earthquakes and boilings of the earth, and from heaven thunders and forked lightnings and frightful thunderbolts and brightness seen in the sky, and fierce gales and floods of rain and torrents. Furthermore there were irregular movements of unusual stars, their wandering courses, and again their disappearances, and still others again fixed in position but for long periods pouring out smoke. And many other such marvelous and unusual signs showed the Divine power presaging the future and suggesting a new order of things and a complete change. For pictures sweated in the churches, as did pillars, and statues of holy men. There were instances of supernatural possession or inspiration of men and women which boded no good, and the soothsayers prophesied many misfortunes. Old prophecies and oracles were recalled and repeated, and every sort of thing which is likely to happen under such circumstances, all took place, all pointing to no good. These all brought great terror and agony to people, totally confounded them, and gave no hope for the future.

§ 96. Still, as if rousing themselves a little in the midst

35

of these evils, they made preparation as they were able. They cleared out the moats, repaired the breaches in the walls, armed the battlements, built up towers and breastworks, and strengthened the whole wall, both on the landward side and along the sea. Furthermore they collected arms, arrows, and every sort of weapon; and they provided the points outside the fortifications with weapons and garrisons, and also fortified the islands.

§ 97. After that, they closed up the great harbor with long chains, the whole Golden Horn from the Arsenal in Galata over to the Gate of Eugenius, which was the narrowest point. And they collected moneys from public funds, private sources, and from the churches. They also provided wheat and other foodstuffs, and in every other way they made what preparation they could, and got ready the armaments for the City and for its walls, knowing that they would be besieged by land and by sea.

§ 98. In addition to this, they sent ambassadors everywhere, wherever they had the least hope of aid, some to the Peloponnesus, to the Despots⁷ there, asking for grain, and for helpers; for they thought this aid might be furnished them eventually, and they did not expect that the City would be taken by assault and by force of arms, as it actually was. They also sent to the great High Priest of Rome [the Pope], from whom they had still more hope, and also to the other princes of Italy and of the other western nations, begging them to grant to them as soon as possible their alliance and aid, if indeed they would take the risk, for they were already in the greatest danger. This was the situation of the one party.

§ 99. But Sultan Mehmed, since he was already carrying on the war brilliantly against the foes outside the City, attacking and scattering some, plundering and dispersing others, and subduing still others, now prepared to attack the City itself in the early spring, by land and by sea. He first collected his forces and drilled them, gathering his armies from all parts, from Asia and from Europe, cavalry and infantry. Also heavy infantry and bowmen and lancers and slingers were

---

⁷ Demetrios and Thomas Palaeologus, brothers of Constantine XIII and governors of the remaining Byzantine territories in the Peloponnesus.

enlisted, and he reviewed all the other units. He also prepared armor for the protection of those in the front line of battle: shields, helmets, breastplates, and great oblong shields lined on the outside with iron; arrows, javelins, swords, and whatever else was thought suitable for fighting against a walled city. He did all this with great haste. Besides these, he devised machines of all sorts against this wall, among others various stone-throwers and especially the newest kind, a strange sort, unbelievable when told of but, as experience demonstrated, able to accomplish everything.

§100. Above all, he prepared the fleet, building some new triremes, repairing others that were damaged by time, and drying out and caulking those that leaked. In addition, he built long ships, heavily armed and swift, with thirty to fifty rowers, and he prepared and arranged everything else necessary for the equipment of these as quickly as possible, sparing nothing that would serve this end.

§ 101. Furthermore, he chose crews from all his coast-towns, Asiatic and European: rowers, overseers, pilots, and those who should serve on the decks, also captains and boat-swains, trireme commanders, commanders of the sailing ships, and admirals, and the rest of the crews for the ships. He accomplished this with great care and speed, for he attached greater importance, for the siege and for fighting, to the fleet than to the army. He therefore gave more of his attention to it, and used all haste and earnestness, and also zeal, for this purpose. For he thought this was of special advantage to him.

Great activity of the Sultan against the City by land and sea

§ 102. While he was so engaged, making preparations throughout the winter, spring began to appear. Immediately he prepared the ships to start out from Gallipoli, for there they were all assembled. And he put in command as Admiral over them, Baltaoglou, the Governor of Gallipoli. The total number of ships was said to be three hundred and fifty without counting the transports or those engaged in some other necessary service. They set sail with great speed, and with shouts and noise and cheers, and they sang rowing chanties and urged one another to emulation by shouts.

§ 103. When they left the Hellespont, they created the greatest possible astonishment and fear among all who saw them. Nowhere for a very long time had such a large fleet of ships or such great preparations by sea been made. Most of all did this astound the unfortunate Romans [Byzantines], for it was so much greater than they had anticipated, and it reduced them to abject despair and took away every last ray of hope from them. On former occasions, whenever enemies had attacked them, they had been besieged only by land but had held the seas and could get the necessities in abundance by using their maritime commerce. Hence they had borne the war easily and withstood the attacks without difficulty, having many means of help, since the enemy was attacking only on one side, from the land. But now, seeing war approaching both by land and by sea, quite naturally they were terrified and greatly dismayed, and were a prey to terrible fear.

§ 104. The Sultan himself set out from Adrianople with all his army, cavalry and infantry, moving along across country, devastating and disturbing everything, causing panic and agony and the greatest dismay wherever he went. He brought with him also the machines [cannon], and in ten days he reached Byzantium. He encamped before the City, rather near the walls, about four stadia off, opposite the gate called the Gate of Romanos.

§ 105. Now the ships came to anchor here and there along the shore, opposite the City, filling all the coast, while the entire army was, as it was stated, more than three hundred thousand fighters without counting the other multitude, a very large one, of camp-followers.

§ 106. The Romans [Byzantines], seeing such a great force, both military and naval, and such vast preparations going on by land and sea, were astonished at the unheard-of sight and at the immensity of the attack. But they on their part by no means neglected preparation for the fight and counter-measures. Instead, they did everything, neglecting nothing. First they moored great galleons near the chain at the mouth of the great harbor, in close array and with bows forward, then long triremes around these in order to prevent by this means the entry of the enemy's ships.

§ 107. There happened also to be present at that time triremes from Italy, six Venetian ships, not come for war, but for a special duty and also great galleons from Crete, coming for trade. And these they persuaded to accede to their demand and stay for the battle.

Arrival of the Italian Giustinianni in the City with his ships to help

§ 108. During these same days there arrived also a certain Italian gentleman, Justin by name,[8] a powerful man and of the nobility, and also experienced in matters of war and extremely gallant, having with him two of the large galleons which he had of his own accord equipped and armed well, with men and with all sorts of arms. He had on the decks four hundred men in full armor. He had stopped near Chios and Rhodes and that part of the sea, recruiting more men from there.

§ 109. This man, when he learned of the war against the Romans and of the impending siege of the City and of the great preparations of Sultan Mehmed against it, came of his own accord with his galleons to help the Romans and the Emperor Constantine. There are those who say that he was asked to come by Constantine, who promised him, after the war, the island of Lemnos as a reward for his help.

§ 110. This man in a short time gave proof of his sagacity and cleverness, and was given great marks of confidence. He was received and brilliantly honored by the Emperor, the nobles, and the city government, and was appointed military dictator and chief of the whole war, including things both under and beyond the control of the laws. He was also put in charge of the weapons and every necessity and preparation for war. On his appointment, he made all sorts of repairs in the City, armed all the land walls, and furnished the battlements with catapults and all sorts of weapons. He also gave

---

8 Giovanni Longo di Giustinianni, a Genoese.

careful instructions to those in the front line and to their scouts, and placed each one of them where he ought to be, and instructed them how they must resist the attackers and defend the wall.

§ 111. He also fortified the harbor walls, as I said, with galleons and triremes and all sorts of machines, and he abundantly supplied the entire sea wall with arms, as he had the land walls. This man was experienced in war, as I stated, and was especially trained in wall-fighting.

§ 112. He designated for himself that part of the wall opposite the encampment of the Sultan, as being a good place for fighting. There was the finest part of the [Ottoman] army, and the imperial guard and the court, and there the attackers planned to bring their cannon into action. So he chose to lead the fighting there, and to join battle and to defend the wall with his own body-guard. For he had with him, as I have just said, four hundred men in armor, not counting the rest of the ships' crews.

§ 113. At that juncture there was a brief sortie from the City against some from the besieging army who had attacked in irregular formation, and they killed some of them and wounded a few. But after encountering a larger force in a counter-attack from the [Ottoman] army, they took refuge in the City, closed the gates, and did not sally forth again but simply guarded the City.

§ 114. Sultan Mehmed pitched his camp somewhere near the place called Mesoteichion,[9] and Myriandrion, not far from the wall, but as near as possible, only out of range of the arrows. He first judged it wise to use conciliatory words toward the Romans, to the effect that if they were willing to deliver over the City and themselves to him with agreements and solemn oaths they might live with their wives and children and all their belongings in safety, suffering no evils and carrying on their business in peace. He sent men to make these proposals, and they on their arrival delivered the Sultan's message.

§ 115. The Romans, however, would not accept such con-

[9] "The Middle of the Wall"—the low-lying region between Top Kapu and Edirne Kapu.

ditions. They said they were willing to make another sort of treaty, but that they could not surrender the City to him.

§ 116. When the Sultan heard this, he immediately laid waste the country and devastated all the parts around the City. After that he took with him Zaganos and Halil, men of the highest rank, and with them others of the generals, and went along the landward side of the City, reconnoitering the wall on that side to see where it was most vulnerable to attack and where it was impregnable, and where he must place the cannon so as to shatter it.

Review of the whole army, and the assignment of the parts of the City on landward and seaward sides to the generals by the Sultan

§ 117. After this, he reviewed the whole army and gave to the governors and cavalry captains and generals of divisions and chiefs of battalions, to each his orders, assigning the stations where they must guard and fight and giving them directions what to do. And he divided the whole City into parts, the land-walls and the sea-walls. To Zaganos and his men with certain others of the captains, he entrusted the siege of Galata and the region all around it, with the Horn and the entire harbor, going as far as what is called the "Wooden Gate" of the City. He ordered him to make a bridge across that part of the Horn, from Ceramica [The Brick-kilns] to the other side. Opposite them was the wall of the City. He knew that by sending the heavy infantry and the bowmen across this bridge, he could attack the City from every point, and so would make the siege complete.

§ 118. To Karaja, the Governor of Europe, and to others of the generals, he committed the section from the Wooden Gate going up toward the Palace of Porphyrogenitus and extending to what is known as the Gate of Charisus; and he gave him some of the cannon, accompanied by the founders who had cast them, to bombard the wall at that point, if perchance it might be weak and vulnerable and he might knock it down.

§ 119. And he assigned to Ishak, the Governor of Asia at

that time, and to Mahmud, the Count of that region, brave men and men of remarkable experience and daring in battle, the section from Myriandrion to the Golden Gate and the sea at that point.

§ 120. The Sultan himself, with the two Pashas, Halil and Karaja, took over the middle of the City and of the land-wall, where he certainly expected there would be the most of the fighting. He had with him the whole imperial guard, by which I mean the best of the infantry and the bowmen and the aides-de-camp and the rest of his personal forces, which were the finest in the army.

§ 121. When he had thus deployed his land forces, and had secured the wall in every section by means of them, and had hemmed it in with his army, he entrusted the fighting by sea to Baltaoglou, a brave man, experienced in all sorts of maritime enterprises, and a skilled commander, whom he appointed Admiral of the whole fleet, and of all the shore, both Asiatic and European. He was the governor of Gallipoli. This man blockaded the entire sea-wall with his ships, from the Golden Gate at the corner as far as the Neorion region of Galata, a distance of just about forty-three stadia. The blockade included the chain and the fighting-ships and galleons anchored by it.

§ 122. It was at this chain that he attacked daily, and he pushed the fighting, being desirous of forcing an entrance into the harbor, so that he might carry the battle to the whole of the wall along the Horn.

§ 123. The entire circuit of the City as besieged by the army by land and sea, carefully calculated, was about 126 stadia; of this, only the wall along the Horn, inside the chain, was unguarded—35 stadia; all the rest was defended.

§ 124. Having done all this, the Sultan summoned the cannon-makers and spoke to them about the cannon and the walls, and about how the wall could most easily be demolished. They assured him it would be easy to demolish it if, in addition to the guns they already had (for they already had some others, made earlier), they should construct one more, which, they believed, would be strong enough to batter down and destroy the wall. For this, heavy expense was needed, to

42

purchase both a large amount of brass and many other materials.

Statement as to the Construction of the cannon, and as to its shape and power

§ 125. No sooner said than done. The Sultan immediately provided them in abundancé with everything they needed, and so they constructed the cannon, a thing most fearsome to see and altogether unbelievable and hard to accept when one hears about it. I shall describe its construction, its appearance, and its power, as it really was.

§ 126. Clay was mixed for many days, so as to make it very workable, made of the lightest, cleanest and finest earth. It was thoroughly mixed together and mingled with linen, hemp, and other such things combined and worked in, after having been chopped up fine, so as to form one body, continuous and inseparable.

§ 127. Of this, a round model was constructed like a pipe, oblong, to be the core. The length of this was forty spans. Of this the forward half, for the reception of the stone cannonball, was of twelve spans as the circle and circumference of its thickness; while the hinder half, or tail, for the reception of the substance called "fodder" was of four spans or slightly more, as the circumference of its thickness, in proportion, I believe, to the whole.

§ 128. There was also another, an outer casing, made to receive this, altogether hollow, and like a scabbard, but wider, so as to fit over the core and leave some space between. And the space between the core and the casing, uniform throughout the whole length, was of one span, or a little more. It was to receive the bronze poured out from the crucible to form the body of the cannon. And this outer mold was made of the same clay, but was completely bound around and protected by iron and wood and earth and stones built up and reinforced from outside, so that the great weight of the bronze bearing down within, might not break it apart or spoil the form of the cannon.

§ 129. Two furnaces were then built, very near to the

mold, ready for the foundry, very strong and reliable, made on the inside with burnt brick and of clay well worked and hardened, and on the outside completely strengthened with immense stones, lime, and everything else suitable for this purpose.

§ 130. Of bronze and tin an amount of great value and of great weight was cast into the foundries—in fact, 1500 talents, as was reported. Besides, a great quantity of charcoal and of tree-trunks was heaped up on the outside of the crucibles, above and below and all around, to such a depth as to hide the furnaces, all but their mouths.

§ 131. Around them were bellows blowing violently and continuously, setting fire to the whole mass for three whole days and as many nights, until the bronze was entirely melted and dissolved, becoming liquid and fluid.

§ 132. Then, when the mouths were opened, the bronze poured out through the conduits into the mold until the whole receptacle was completely full, and it covered the inner core entirely, and overflowed this by a cubit in height; and thus was the cannon completed. After that, when the bronze had cooled off and become cold, it was cleared of both the inner core and the outer casing, and being smoothed and polished by scrapers, it shone altogether. Such was the construction and the form of the cannon.

§ 133. And now I will speak of its method of working. First, what is called "fodder" [powder] was put in, filling up tightly the rear compartment and cavity of the machine up to the opening of the second compartment which was to receive the stone cannon-ball. Then there was put in a huge rod of strongest wood, and this, pounded hard by iron bars, pressed down on the material inside, closing in and packing down the powder so completely that, whatever happened, nothing could force it out in any way except by an explosion.

§ 134. Then they brought the stone also, pushing it in until they used the rod and fitted the stone in snugly on all sides.

§ 135. After this, having pointed the cannon toward whatever it was intended to hit, and having leveled it by certain technical means and calculations toward the target, they brought up great beams of wood and laid them underneath and fitted them carefully. On these they placed immense stones, weighting it down and making it secure above and below and behind and everywhere, lest by the force of the velocity and by the shock of the movement of its own emplacement, it should be displaced and shoot wide of its mark.

§ 136. Then they set fire to it through the short hole behind, igniting the powder. And when this took fire, quicker than it takes to say it, there was a fearful roar first, and a shaking of the earth beneath and for a long way off, and a noise such as never was heard before. Then, with an astounding thunder and a frightful crashing and a flame that lit up all the surroundings and then left them black, the rod, forced out from within by a dry hot blast of air, violently set in motion the stone as it came out. And the stone, borne with tremendous force and velocity, hit the wall, which it immediately shook and knocked down, and was itself broken into many fragments and scattered, hurling the pieces everywhere and killing those who happened to be near by.

§ 137. Sometimes it demolished a whole section, and sometimes a half-section, and sometimes a larger or smaller section of a tower or turret or battlement. And there was no part of the wall strong enough or resistant enough or thick enough to be able to withstand it, or to wholly resist such force and such a blow of the stone cannon-ball.

§ 138. Such was the unbelievable and inconceivable nature of the power of this implement. Such a thing, the ancients, whether kings or generals, neither had nor knew about. Had they possessed it, nothing could have withstood them at all, nor stood up against them in their sieges; nor would it have been difficult for them to topple over and destroy walls. Even the best fortified of them would have offered no obstacle. They built walls, and dug intrenchments, and mined under the earth, and did all sorts of other things so as to secure possession of cities and capture forts, but all these would have surrendered quicker than it takes to tell it, if shattered and overthrown by these machines. But they had none.

§ 139. This is a new invention of the Germans or Kelts, about a hundred fifty years ago or a little more—a very wise

45

and ingenious invention. Especially the composition and formation of "fodder," which is a combination of the very warmest and driest forms of nitre, sulphur, carbon, and herbs, making a dry and warm gas, which, being enclosed in the impervious, strong, compact body of the bronze and not having any other exit of any sort anywhere except this one, is impelled by the explosion and force from within and gives so great and powerful a force to the stone ball. But it also frequently causes the bursting of the bronze as well. Now no ancient name is found for this machine, unless someone may speak of it as the *battering-ram* or the *propeller*. But in common language everybody today calls it an *apparatus*. Such are the details about the cannon, as far as we have been able to learn from those who could inform us.

§ 140. Sultan Mehmed, since the makers of the cannon had completed them successfully, ordered them to bring the cannon near the walls. Over against the Middle Wall where he had his camp, and where his tent was, he ordered them to set up three of them, chosen as the largest and most powerful, and to bombard and shake the wall at that point. He ordered the others to be brought up against portions of the wall here and there, choosing the most vulnerable and weakest parts of the walls. For he judged it best to attack the wall at many points, so that, after he had begun the battle in several places, the capture of it would prove easier and more facile for him, as indeed it turned out to be.

§ 141. And the cannon, on being brought up to the wall, shook it to pieces and toppled it down as they were expected to.

§ 142. Then the Sultan filled up the moat in front of the cannon, bringing up stones and wood and earth and collecting every other sort of material so that when the wall was battered down and had fallen, the way should be easier for the heavy infantry, and their approach and attack facilitated. And he ordered the sappers to dig underneath the wall, and to dig subterranean galleries in toward the City, so that the heavy infantry might get in secretly by night through these. This work also went forward, but later he deemed this superfluous

46

and a useless expenditure, since the cannon were accomplishing everything.

Arrival of the Sultan at the fort of Therapia, and its capture in two days

§ 143. While these events were occurring, the Sultan took some of the troops with him, including the entire Royal Guard, and went against the particularly strong fortress at Therapia. Having set up some cannon, he battered down and destroyed the greater part of it. Of the men within many died from the stone cannon-balls, while the rest of the defenders, unable to resist any longer, surrendered, saying he might do as he pleased with them. So he impaled them, being forty men.

Subsequent arrival at the Studius Fort, and the immediate capture of this

§ 144. From there he went against another fort called Studius's Castle. And when he had shattered it with his guns and thrown it down, he immediately entered it and impaled its thirty-six men, bringing them in front of the City wall so that they might be easily visible to those inside the City.

Voyage of Baltaoglou to the Island of Prinkipo; siege and capture of its fort

§ 145. During those same days, Baltaoglou, Admiral of the fleet, left the greater part of his ships to attack the mouth of the harbor and the chain, so that none might sail in or out. He himself, with the rest, then sailed at the command of the Sultan against Prinkipo Island. There was there a very strong castle with a guard of some thirty fully-armed men aside from the local inhabitants. So he besieged it, brought up some cannon against the wall, and shattered and overthrew a part of this. But though he attacked in every way and tried all means, he was as yet unable to capture it.

§ 146. At last he decided to use fire against the fort and

see whether he could burn it down, providing a favorable wind should come up. Hence he ordered his men to gather great bundles of fagots of all sorts, reeds, twigs, weeds, and other inflammable things, and bind them together and place them against the wall. When this had been done in a short time by many hands and the material was heaped up to a great height, they set it on fire, having added brimstone and pitch. And this, being soon ignited by the flames and, as it happened, fanned by a breeze, made such a big flame, blazing up to such a height, that it rose higher than the turrets and caught inside the castle also. It burned up many of those within, and indeed came near destroying them all. The survivors barely escaped, being seriously endangered by the fire. They surrendered unconditionally to him. He took them all prisoners, sold the civilians as slaves, and killed the rest of the guards.

§ 147. Now the Romans [Byzantines] and Giustinianni, seeing the City wall so severely battered and damaged by the guns, both within and without, extended great beams from above the wall, and let down bales of wool on ropes, and placed with them other similar things so as to break the force of the stone balls as much as possible and lighten the effect.

§ 148. But since this proved of use only a short time and accomplished nothing worth mentioning inasmuch as the cannon were piercing and scattering everything and demolishing the wall—for already a large part of the lesser outer wall had fallen and also two towers and a turret of the main wall—they devised another thing. They brought up huge stakes and made a palisade along the damaged part of the wall—that is, on its outer side—fastening the stakes securely together. In addition they brought a quantity of all kinds of stones and wood, bundles of brushwood and branches and reeds and many other bushes of all sorts, putting them together in bundles and so raising the stockade higher. There were also screens, made of skins and hides, put over the wood of the palisade so that it should not be injured by the firebrand arrows. They thus had a fine shelter against the enemy, and a strengthening of the palisade from within, which was in place of a wall. Moreover the stone ball, hurled with great force, fell and was buried in the soft and yielding earth, and did not make a breach by striking against hard and unyielding materials.

§ 149. On the top of the palisade and of the earthworks were placed rows of wooden containers filled with earth, to act as breastworks for the fighters in the forefront and as a protection so that they should not be hit by the arrows.

First Assault attempted by the Sultan against the wall, and its failure

§ 150. When Sultan Mehmed returned from the fortresses, he believed he could after a few days try an assault on the City at the points where the wall had been broken through. Therefore, taking the heavy infantry and the bowmen and javelin-men and all the imperial foot-guards, he made a vigorous attack on the wall. The moat was already filled up, so the foot-soldiers, with shout and battle cry, quickly crossed it and assaulted the wall. First they tried to set fire to the gate, so as to burn the stockade and spread confusion and panic among their opponents in the fight.

§ 151. But since this did not succeed as they had hoped, because the men who were stationed at the top of the stockade fought finely and put out the fire, they changed to another plan. Fastening hooks on the ends of their spears, they pulled down from above the wooden containers and thus stripped the defenders of their shelter. These containers had served them like the crenellations of a wall, but now the archers and slingers and javelin-hurlers could easily attack the undefended enemy. Others brought ladders and put them up against the wall and tried to climb up them while the cannon fired stones frequently against the defenders and did considerable damage.

§ 152. Giustinianni and his men (for they and a considerable number of the Romans also, had been detailed to the damaged part of the wall), since they were fully armored, sustained no injury from the arrows or other missiles. Instead, they stoutly resisted, fighting bravely and using every measure to withstand and frustrate whatever their opponents did.

At last the Romans and Giustinianni prevailed and repulsed them, though not without difficulty, and drove them from the wall, wounding many of them and killing not a few.

§ 153. Other attacks were made daily, here and there, on the wall, especially where it had been demolished. During these attacks the defenders in the City were by no means worsted, but fought vigorously and resisted bravely.

§ 154. Baltaoglou, after capturing the fortress [of Prinkipo], immediately sailed to the harbor where the other triremes were drawn up. On the second or third day he received an order from the Sultan to make careful preparation and collect his ships and join battle with the galleons and triremes that were guarding the mouth of the harbor and the chain, so as to force an entrance if he could. The Sultan had determined by all means to get the harbor and the Horn under his control so that he might attack the City from all sides, by land and by sea, for he thought (as was true) that if he could make an opening in the sea-wall as well, the capture of the City would be easier for him, since the defenders were insufficient for the entire circuit, they being few and the circuit great.

Attack of Baltaoglou against the vessels at the entrance to the harbor, and at the chain; the great sea-battle

§ 155. Having put all the ships in good condition and fully armed them, and the fighting men with them, Baltaoglou attacked the galleons and the chain with great force, fury, and vigor, and with shouts and battle cries. And first, having slowed down the ships, when they were about a bowshot from the enemy, they attacked from afar, firing on them and being fired upon with arrows and with great stone balls from the guns. Then he furiously attacked the center of the fleet. Of the heavy infantry on the decks, some carried fire in their hands with the purpose of setting fire to the ships. Others hurled flaming arrows, while others tried to cut the ropes of the anchors, and still others attempted to board the ships, climbing up by grappling-hooks and ladders. Others with javelins and pikes and long spears attacked the defenders. Their attack and their zeal for the task were very great.

§ 156. Now those on the large galleons had already been prepared for such attack by the Grand Duke, who had been placed in command over the ships as well as of the sea-walls of the City; so, fighting from a higher position, and hurling down on the attackers stones, javelins, spears and pikes, especially from the crowsnests at the top of the masts, they succeeded in wounding many, and killed not a few. Furthermore they brought great jars of water to put out the fires, and heavy stones which they let fall, tied by ropes, and thus did a great deal of damage.

§ 157. There was the greatest zeal on both sides, and energy too, the attackers determined to prevail and to force their way in while the defenders were bound to fight their best to guard the harbor and the ships and drive off the enemy. At last the crews of the galleons, fighting magnificently, turned the flank of the attackers and drove them off, having proved themselves valiant men to the very end.

The invention of another and newer sort of cannon

§ 158. Sultan Mehmed, seeing that he had been repulsed in this attack, set himself to discover another sort of machine. Hence, calling the makers of the cannon, he demanded of them whether it was not possible to fire cannon-balls at the galleons fighting at the entrance to the harbor, and sink them there. They replied that they were unable to do this, especially because the walls of Galata were in the way at every point. He then showed them another way to do this by a new form of cannon. For, he said, if they were willing, it was possible to construct a different sort of gun with a slightly changed design that could fire the stone to a great height, so that when it came down it would hit the ships amidships and sink them. He said that they must first aim it and level it, getting the measures by mathematical calculation, and then fire on the galleons. Thus he explained to them his plan.

§ 159 When they had reasoned out the scheme, they decided it was possible. So they constructed a cannon of this type, as designed by the Sultan, and after a careful survey of the land, they placed it a little beyond the point of Galata on a slight elevation opposite the galleons. Then having aimed it with care, and after leveling it by a special design, they fired it by applying a live coal to it. It shot the stone up to a great height, but as this first stone descended, it missed the ships, falling into the sea quite near them. However, when they had immediately corrected the error by changing the aim a little, they fired again, and this stone went to an immense height and came down with tremendous crash and velocity, striking the galleon in the center. It immediately crushed it completely and sank it in the depths, killing some of those on board immediately and drowning others. The very few who were not killed swam with difficulty to the other galleons and triremes near by.

§ 160. This unexpected event frightened all those in the City, and threw them into the greatest terror and anguish. Nonetheless, since this was the only possible safe step, the rest of the galleons and triremes were retired a short distance to a safer place, and a guard was set. Thus they suffered no further injury from the cannon-balls, but strongly guarded the harbor and the Horn.

§ 161. While affairs were in this condition, not more than three or four days later, three large galleons appeared in the open sea sailing grandly along. The High Priest of Rome [the Pope] had sent these from Italy, bringing food and help to the City. He had already learned of the fighting and of the approaching siege of the City, so he had sent these ahead as help until he should fit out the rest of his fleet as well. He was preparing to send from Italy thirty triremes and galleons after these, as aid to the Romans and the Emperor Constantine, but these were delayed.

§ 162. When the enemy saw these galleons sailing out in the open sea, they gave word to the Sultan, who immediately sent for Baltaoglou, Commander of the fleet, and ordered him to put out with the entire fleet as quickly as possible, putting on a full complement of rowers and others on all the ships and fighters on the decks, and arming them with every sort of weapon. He also put on board the ships many other weapons: shields, cutlasses, helmets, breastplates, also javelins, pikes, long spears, daggers, and whatever else was usable in this kind of fight. Furthermore he provided the ships with as many heavy infantry and bowmen as he could, and from his own bodyguard the best fighters, the bravest in battle, and those best armed. So, after equipping and preparing the fleet with plenty of men and all sorts of arms, he sent it out, ordering them either to capture the galleons and bring them to him or else never to come back safe themselves.

Attack by the Sultan's fleet on the ships that appeared in the open sea; severe naval battle and failure

§ 163. Baltaoglou took the entire fleet and started immediately against the transports in all haste and zealously, and also with ambition and hope of success. He almost imagined that they were already in his hands. When they came within range of his arrows, they first lay to for a little while, and then he had very lively skirmishes, with arrows and with stones hurled by his cannon and even with flaming arrows against the sails and the galleons, with the purpose of setting them on fire.

§ 164. The men on the galleons also fought bravely. They attacked from a height, and in fact from the yardarms and the wooden towers they fired down with arrows, javelins and stones, impetuously and indeed successfully. There was much shouting, and men were wounded and killed on both sides.

§ 165. When they had kept on in that way for a time, Baltaoglou set up a great shout and ordered the rest to do so too. Then with great speed and force he attacked the center of the galleons, and there followed a hand-to-hand fight as both sides attacked with small-arms. Altogether it was a terrible struggle. Some carried fire and tried to set the galleons ablaze from below. Others with axes and daggers tried to break through their sidewalls, while others with long lances and javelins shot at the warriors from below. Some hurled pikes and stones, and others climbed up, clinging to anchors and ropes, and tried to get aboard the ships. So in various ways they fought, wounding and being wounded, in ferocity and anger.

§ 166. The men on board the galleons were fully armed and fought desperately against them from their higher position, defending themselves energetically against the attackers. First they emptied great vessels of water which they had hung over the sides, and dropped down from above heavy stones that they had tied with ropes. Thus they put out the fire and killed many. The stones, falling heavily and with great force on all who were attacking from below, sank some boats and injured others. After that, some of them hurled spears and javelins and pikes on the attackers, others threw stones from above, while others with their cutlasses cut off the hands of those who tried to board. Still others beat down with clubs and sticks and broke the heads of those men by their blows. There was great shouting and din on all sides as they encouraged each other, hitting and being hit, killing and being killed, pushing and being pushed, blaspheming, scolding, threatening, groaning—it was all a terrible noise.

§ 167. And yet, although the men in the galleons struggled bravely, those in the fleet were getting the better of them through sheer force of numbers, for they fought by turns, relieving one another, fresh ones taking the places and work of those who had been wounded or killed. And those on the galleons would have lost hope of fighting successfully, because the battle had gone on so long, had not a south wind, suddenly coming up strong, blown into the bellying sails and powerfully swelled them out and driven the galleons along with great force. In a brief time they left behind the triremes, which could not keep up with the galleons. Therefore the fight died down, and they got safely away to the other galleons at the entrance of the harbor, and thus, in spite of their fears, were saved. They escaped a very great danger.

§ 168. The Sultan, seated on his horse by the shore, watched these events and seemed to be encouraging his men as well as watching the outcome of the battle. For he felt absolutely sure his fleet would defeat the galleons and capture them and bring them as captives to him, and he was in great glee. But when he saw the wind freshening, and the galleons drawing away, he was immediately greatly chagrined. Whipping up his horse, he went off in silence.

§ 169. Of the men in the galleons, universal testimony says twenty-two were killed, but more than half of the men in their complements were wounded.

§ 170. Of the men in the Sultan's fleet, a little more than a hundred were killed, and the wounded were more than three hundred. Baltaoglou, the admiral of the fleet, was hit in the eye with a stone. This contributed both to the safety of the galleons and to the saving of Baltaoglou himself from death by order of the Sultan, for the latter took very hard the escape of the galleons, and felt very badly at the affair, accusing Baltaoglou of cowardice and pusillanimity. Rather, he thought the outcome due to the admiral's carelessness and idleness, and that the admiral had betrayed his plans. For he did not consider the failure in the matter of the galleons was a good omen for the task he had before him. Hence he relieved the admiral of the command immediately and gave the fleet and the governorship of Gallipoli to Hamza, one of his companions whom he greatly trusted in such affairs.

§ 171. On the other hand, this unhoped-for outcome brought to the Romans more than a little respite and encouragement and filled them with better hopes, not only at what had occurred but also in expectation of better things to come—until they had to suffer badly. The evils had not yet come upon them. They were not to be happy for any length of time; they were to be captured, and given over to all sorts of evil, to captivity and slavery, murder, plunder, and the abuse of women and children.

A Surprising Plan and Decision

§ 172. Sultan Mehmed considered it necessary in preparation for his next move to get possession of the harbor and open the Horn for his own ships to sail in. So, since every effort and device of his had failed to force the entrance, he made a wise decision, and one worthy of his intellect and power. It succeeded in accomplishing his purpose and in putting an end to all uncertainties.

§ 173. He ordered the commanders of the vessels to construct as quickly as possible glideways leading from the outer sea to the inner sea, that is, from the harbor to the Horn, near the place called Diplokion, and to cover them with beams. This road, measured from sea to sea, is just about eight stadia. It is very steep for more than half the way, until you reach the summit of the hill, and from there again it descends to the inner sea of the Horn. And as the glideways were completed sooner than expected, because of the large number of workers, he brought up the ships and placed large cradles under them, with stays against each of their sides to hold them up. And having under-girded them well with ropes, he fastened long cables to the corners and gave them to the soldiers to drag, some of them by hand, and others by certain machines and capstans.

§ 174. So the ships were dragged along very swiftly. And their crews, as they followed them, rejoiced at the event and boasted of it. Then they manned the ships on the land as if they were on the sea. Some of them hoisted the sails with a shout, as if they were setting sail, and the breeze caught the sails and bellied them out. Others seated themselves on the benches, holding the oars in their hands and moving them as if rowing. And the commanders, running along by the sockets of the masts with whistlings and shouting, and with their whips beating the oarsmen on the benches, ordered them to row. The ships, borne along over the land as if on the sea, were some of them being pulled up the ascent to the top of the hill while others were being hauled down the slope into the harbor, lowering the sails with shouting and great noise.

§ 175. It was a strange spectacle, and unbelievable in the telling except to those who actually did see it—the sight of ships borne along on the mainland as if sailing on the sea, with their crews and their sails and all their equipment. I believe this was a much greater feat than the cutting of a canal across at Athos by Xerxes, and much stranger to see and to hear about. Furthermore, this event of but yesterday, before our very eyes, makes it easier to believe that the other also actually happened, for without this one, the other would have seemed a myth and sounded like idle talk.

§ 176. Thus, then, there was assembled in the bay called Cold Waters, a little beyond Galata, a respectable fleet of some sixty-seven vessels. They were moored there.

§ 177. The Romans, when they saw such an unheard-of thing actually happen, and warships lying at anchor in the Horn—which they never would have suspected—were astounded at the impossibility of the spectacle, and were overcome by the greatest consternation and perplexity. They did not know what to do now, but were in despair. In fact they had left unguarded the walls along the Horn for a distance of about thirty stadia, and even so they did not have enough men for the rest of the walls, either for defense or for attack, whether citizens or men from elsewhere. Instead, two or even three battlements had but a single defender.

§ 178. And now, when this sea-wall also became open to attack and had to be guarded, they were compelled to strip the other battlements and bring men there. This constituted a manifest danger, since the defenders were taken away from the rest of the wall while those remaining were not enough to guard it, being so few.

§ 179. Not only was there this difficulty, but, the bridge being completed, heavy infantry and bowmen could cross against the wall. Hence that part also had to be guarded. And the ships near the mouth of the harbor and at the chain, galleons and triremes alike, as well as the other ships in the harbor had the greater need to be on guard since now they were subject to attack from within as well as from outside. Therefore in many directions they appeared to have, and actually had, difficulties. Still, they did not neglect anything that could be done.

§ 180. Giustinianni removed one of his galleons from the mouth of the harbor plus three of the Italian triremes, and took them against the end of the gulf where the Sultan's ships were anchored. There he anchored so as to fight from them and prevent the [Ottoman] warships from going out anywhere in the gulf or being able to do any harm to the harbor or its shipping. This he thought was the best plan as a counter-measure. But it was only a temporary expedient.

§ 181. For Sultan Mehmed, seeing this, made the following counter-moves: He ordered the cannon-makers to transfer the cannon secretly by night and place them near the shore, opposite to where the ships and the galleon were moored, and fire stones at them. This they did with great speed, and they hit one of the triremes in the middle and sank it with all on board, excepting a very few who swam to the other triremes. Then the crews quickly moved the ships away a good distance, and anchored there. If this had not been done quickly, the other triremes also would have been sunk, with their crews, as well as the galleon, for they seemed to have had no sense at all of their danger. They were thus very near to destruction, for the cannon were ready to fire the stone balls at them.

§ 182. But when this failed, the Romans had nothing else they could do. They simply fired at the ships from the walls with catapults and javelins and prevented them from moving about. And from the triremes at the mouth of the harbor some attacked them every day and chased them back and prevented their injuring anything in the harbor. And they often pursued them till near the land, toward their own men. Then these ships would again turn and attack the triremes, and men would follow on foot, firing and being fired on, and so they had long-range exchanges daily.

Of Some Marvels

§ 183. During those same days there occurred the following divine signs and portents of the terrors that were very soon to come to the city. Three or four days before the battle, when all the people in the City were holding a religious procession, men and women together, and marching around with the Ikon of the Mother of God, this latter slipped suddenly from the hands of its bearers without any cause or power being apparent, and fell flat on the ground. And when everybody shouted immediately, and rushed to raise up the ikon, it sank down as if weighted with lead, and as if fastened to the ground, and became well-nigh impossible to raise. And so it continued for a considerable time, until, by a great effort and much shouting and prayers by all, the priests and its bearers barely managed to raise it up and place it on the shoulders of the men.

§ 184. This strange occurrence filled everyone with much terror and very great agony and fear, for they thought this fall was no good omen—as was quite true. Later, when they had gone on but a short distance, immediately after that, at high noon, there was much thunder and lightning with clouds, and a violent rain with severe hail followed, so that they could neither stand against it nor make any progress. The priests and the bearers of the ikon and the crowds that followed were depressed and hindered by the force of the waters that flowed down and by the might of the hail. Many of the children following were in danger of being carried away and drowned by the violent and powerful rush of water, had not some men quickly seized them and with some difficulty dragged them out of the flood. Such was the unheard-of and unprecedented violence of that storm and hail which certainly foreshadowed the imminent loss of all, and that, like a torrent of fiercest waters, it would carry away and annihilate everything.

Still another portent

§ 185. Such, then, were the events of the first day. On the next day in the morning a dense fog covered the whole city, lasting from early morning till evening. This evidently indicated the departure of the Divine Presence, and its leaving the City in total abandonment and desertion, for the Divinity conceals itself in cloud and appears and again disappears. So then, this happened thus and let no one disbelieve, for there were many witnesses of these things, observers who were both visitors and dwellers in the City.

§ 186. For Sultan Mehmed, then, all went well. There was as yet no hindrance, for both the inner wall and the outer one had been wrecked to the ground by the cannon; the whole moat was filled up; the Horn and all the wall along its shores had been opened up for battle by brilliant tactics; and the siege was complete all around the City, with ladders, wooden towers, and all the rest well prepared. And the siege had lasted quite a while, for nearly fifty days had passed. But there was fear lest something might happen, or that help might appear by sea from somewhere. The Sultan had already heard that a convoy of ships had arrived in Chios, so he knew he had better not delay any longer or wait further, but should join battle quickly and try to capture the City with all speed and with all his force, by an attack by land and sea, and make this greatest and final attempt on it.

§ 187. So he called together all the high officers and those in his entourage, namely: the governors, generals, cavalry officers, majors and captains, the captains over a thousand, over a hundred, and over fifty, and the sub-officers of his soldiers and the cavalry of his body-guard; also besides these, the captains of the heavy transports and of the triremes, and the Admiral of the whole fleet; and he made the following speech.

Second Address of the Sultan, calling upon all to fight bravely, and promising them that they would be rewarded with goods and many other fine things, if they fought well

§ 188. "My friends and my comrades in the present struggle! I have called you together here, not because I would accuse you of any laziness or carelessness in this business, nor try to make you more eager in the present struggle. For a long time past I have noted some of you showing such zeal and earnestness for the work that you would willingly undergo everything necessary rather than leave here without accomplishing it, and others of you not only zealous themselves but even inciting the rest with all their might to redouble their efforts.

§ 189. "So it is not for this that I have called you together, but simply in order to remind you, first of all, that whatever you have at present you have attained, not by sloth and carelessness, but by hard work and with great struggles and dangers together with us, and these things are yours as the rewards of your own valor and manliness rather than as gifts of fortune. And secondly, as to the rewards now put before you here, I wish to show you how many and how great they are and what great glory and honor accompany the winning. And I also wish that you may know well how to carry on the struggle for the very highest rewards.

§ 190. "First, then, there is great wealth of all sorts in this city, some in the royal palaces and some in the houses of the mighty, some in the homes of the common people and still other, finer and more abundant, laid up in the churches as votive offerings and treasures of all sorts, constructed of gold and silver and precious stones and costly pearls. Also there is countless wealth of magnificent furniture, without reckoning all the other articles and furnishings of the houses. Of all these, you will be the masters!

§ 191. "Then too, there are very many noble and distinguished men, some of whom will be your slaves, and the rest will be put up for sale; also very many and very beautiful women, young and good-looking, and virgins lovely for marriage, noble, and of noble families, and even till now unseen by masculine eyes, some of them, evidently intended for the weddings of great men. Of these, some will be wives for you, while others will do for servants, and others you can sell. So you will gain in many ways, in enjoyment, and service, and wealth.

§ 192. "And you will have boys, too, very many and very beautiful and of noble families.

§ 193. "Further, you will enjoy the beauty of the churches and public buildings and splendid houses and gardens, and many such things, suited to look at and enjoy and take pleasure in and profit by. But I must not waste time listing all these. A great and populous city, the capital of the ancient Romans, which has attained the very pinnacle of good fortune and luck and glory, being indeed the head of the whole inhabited globe—I give it now to you for spoil and plunder—unlimited wealth, men, women, children, all the other adornments and arrangements. All these you will enjoy as if at a brilliant banquet, and will be happy with them yourselves and will leave very great wealth to your children.

§ 194. "And the greatest of all is this, that you will capture a city whose renown has gone out to all parts of the world. It is evident that to whatever extent the leadership and glory of this city has spread, to a like extent the renown of your valor and bravery will spread for having captured by assault a city such as this. But think: what deed more brilliant, what greater enjoyment, or what inheritance of wealth better than that presented to you, along with honor and glory!

§ 195. "And, best of all, we shall demolish a city that has been hostile to us from the beginning and is constantly growing at our expense and in every way plotting against our rule. So for the future we shall be sure of guarding our present belongings and shall live in complete and assured peace, after getting rid of our neighboring enemies. We shall also open the way to further conquest.

§ 196. "You must never imagine that, although this is all true, the City is impregnable or its wall hard to approach and difficult to pierce, or that very great danger awaits those who attack it, as if it were not easily to be taken. Lo, as you can see, the moat has all been filled up and the land-wall at three points has been so broken down that not only heavy and light infantry like yourselves, but even the horses and heavily armed cavalry can easily penetrate it. Thus I do not offer you an impregnable wall, but a wide plain fit for cavalry for you to cross with your weapons.

§ 197. "And what should I say about our opponents? There are very few of them, and most of these are unarmed and inexperienced in war. For, as I have learned from deserters, they say that there are but two or three men defending a tower, and as many more in the space between towers. Thus it happens that a single man has to fight and defend three or four battlements, and he, too, either altogether unarmed or badly armed.

§ 198. "How then can they do anything against such a multitude as we are? And especially since we are fighting by relays, and new troops are constantly coming into the fray, so that our men have time to indulge in sleep and food and to rest themselves, while they on the other hand fight continuously, without intermission, and desperately, and have no time to snatch sleep or food or drink or rest, since we are attacking in battle and forcing the fighting. Now we shall no longer merely use skirmishes and sallies, or simple attacks and feints, as we did at first—and as they anticipate—but once we have begun to fight, the battle will be continuous and uninterrupted, night and day, without any rest or armistice until all is up with them. Therefore I think these men, under the constraint of continuous fighting and of distress and starvation and sleeplessness, will easily yield to us.

§ 199. "And as for such Italians as are stationed on the ruined wall, if any think these are seasoned veterans able to defend themselves against the attackers, as though they were well armed and experienced in battle, especially behind fortifications, I, at least, believe the opinion of such persons altogether incredible and mistaken.

§ 200. "In the first place, being intelligent men, they will not be willing to fight on behalf of the goods of others, or suffer and expose themselves to evident risks when they have nothing to gain for themselves. And besides, they are a motley crew, coming from here and there and thinking simply of getting something and going back home in safety, not of dying in battle. For the present they do actually bear it and keep on, because we have been bombarding and attacking only at intervals, and they think that in future also we will go at it as if in child's play.

§ 201. "But when they see the battle rolling in on them, and brilliantly and relentlessly pressed on every side, and death imminent before their eyes, then I am perfectly sure they will not hesitate at all, but will throw away their weapons, turn their backs, and flee, and never turn around. And there will be nothing to deter them or give them courage at all.

§ 202. "But even if by some means they should stand firm, so be it! We will still easily put them to flight by our might and experience and daring. Thus even in that case I do not in the least think we have any good reason at all for worry. All things go to show that victory is on our side, and that we shall capture the City. As you see, it is entirely surrounded, as if in a net, by land and sea; and it cannot finally escape our arms and our grasp.

§ 203. "Then be brave yourselves and urge all the men under you to follow you bravely, and to use all zeal and diligence in the task, in the belief that there are three elements in good fighting: the will to fight, a realization of what is and is not honorable, and obedience to authority. Know that this obedience involves each keeping his own position and going to the attack quietly and in good order so that one can quickly hear the commands given and pass them on to the rest: when they must advance silently, to be silent, when they must shout and yell, to do so with fearsome yells. For while many of these things are wise in every sort of fighting, they are not the least so in battles at the walls. As for the rest, order them all to do everything well and in good order and discipline.

§ 204. "So then, fight bravely and worthily of yourselves and of those who have fought before you; and do not weaken, for you see how much hangs on this struggle, and do not allow any of your men to do so either. I myself will be in the van of the attack [applause by all the gathering]. Yes, I myself will lead the attack, and will be fighting by your side and will watch to see what each one of you does.

§ 205. "Go back, then, each one to his post and his tent, have your supper and rest yourselves. Give like orders to the men in your commands. Then be up early and get your divisions in good order and well arranged, paying no attention to anything outside and listening to no one else. And let the ranks keep silent. But when you hear the battle-cry and see the signal, then get to your jobs!

Position and orders given the generals

§ 206. "You, then, Hamza, sail with your ships along the sea-walls, have some of the ships lie to within shooting range, and order the archers and those who have crossbows in their hands, and muskets, to fire from the decks against the battlements so continuously that no one may lean out at all, nor have a chance to attack in the battle. And run some of the ships aground, if it seems advantageous, by the wall. Then have the men in charge bring out the ladders, and let the infantry try to scale the wall. So fight bravely and show yourself to be a hero.

§ 207. "And you yourself, Zaganos, cross the bridge quickly and attack the Golden Horn wall very vigorously. Take with you the ships inside the harbor, which are assigned to you for this purpose, and be a hero!

§ 208. "Now too you, Karaja, take your men and cross the moat and attack the ruined part of the wall just in front of you. Stoutly hurling back the defenders, try to scale the wall, struggling manfully, like a hero.

§ 209. "And you also, Ishak and Mahmud, cross the moat safely with your own divisions and try to scale the wall with ladders. Have the archers and cannoneers and musketeers shoot incessantly at those on the battlements, so that they may be the least possible hindrance to your attack.

§ 210. "Lastly you, Halil and Saraja, have your troops close ranks on both sides and fight. When you see me struggling and trying to climb up the ruined parts of the wall and forcing the Italians back and opening access for my men into the City, do your utmost on both sides to check those drawn up opposite you, attacking them strongly, so that being given no respite by you they may be less able to pay attention to us, and wholly unable to help those hard pressed by us.

§ 211. "So much for the present. I myself will take care of all the rest. Therefore go back now to your tents and to your troops, and good luck to you! Eat, and drink, and rest."

§ 212. Having said this much, he dismissed the assembly. Each man went to his own troops and tents, and the Sultan himself, after his evening meal, went to rest.

§ 213. Rising at dawn, he first called the gunners and ordered them to make the guns ready and aim them at the wrecked parts of the wall, so that when the time came they might fire on the defenders there.

§ 214. Afterward he summoned the cavalry and infantry of his guard—I mean the heavy infantry and shield-bearers and archers and all the royal guard—and grouped them

effectively by bands, masses, groups, and companies, by
thousands and sometimes in larger numbers. He ordered
them to fight in shifts, when their turns came. Some were to
fight and do battle while others took food and sleep and rested
so that they might be refreshed and renewed for the struggle.
Then those should replace the others, and that thus, with
one division constantly succeeding another and with periods
of rest, the battle should go on incessantly and continuously,
so as to allow their opponents no respite or relaxation in the
fight. He also appointed a place for each, and a time and a
regular order, and commanded them how and where and
when to make their best effort.

§ 215. Then the Sultan mounted his horse and went
around to all the other divisions, reviewing them and giving
his orders to all in general and each in particular. He encouraged them and stirred them up for the battle, especially
the officers of the troops, calling each one by name. Then,
having passed along the entire army, along the wall from sea
to sea, and having given the necessary orders and encouraged
and incited all for the fight, and having urged them to play
the man, he ordered them to have their food and rest until
the battle-cry should be given and they should see the signal.
And after doing all this, he went back to his tent, had his
meal, and rested.

§ 216. Now the Romans, seeing the army so quiet and
more tranquil than usual, marveled at the fact and ventured
on various explanations and guesses. Some—not judging it
aright—thought this was a preparation for withdrawal. Others
—and this proved correct—believed that it was a preparation for battle and an alert, things which they had been expecting in the near future. So they passed the word along
and then went in silence to their own divisions and made all
sorts of preparations.

§ 217. The hour was already advanced, the day was de-
clining and near evening, and the sun was at the Ottomans'
backs but shining in the faces of their enemies. This was
just as the Sultan had wished; accordingly he gave the order
first for the trumpets to sound the battle-signal, and the
other instruments, the pipes and flutes and cymbals too, as

loud as they could. All the trumpets of the other divisions, with the other instruments in turn, sounded all together, a great and fearsome sound. Everything shook and quivered at the noise. After that, the standards were displayed.

§ 218. To begin, the archers and slingers and those in charge of the cannon and the muskets, in accord with the commands given them, advanced against the wall slowly and gradually. When they got within bowshot, they halted to fight. And first they exchanged fire with the heavier weapons, with arrows from the archers, stones from the slingers, and iron and leaden balls from the cannon and muskets. Then, as they closed with battleaxes and javelins and spears, hurling them at each other and being hurled at pitilessly in rage and fierce anger. On both sides there was loud shouting and blasphemy and cursing. Many on each side were wounded, and not a few died. This kept up till sunset, a space of about two or three hours.

§ 219. Then, with fine insight, the Sultan summoned the shield-bearers, heavy infantry and other troops and said: "Go to it, friends and children mine! It is time now to show yourselves good fighters!" They immediately crossed the moat, with shouts and fearful yells, and attacked the outer wall. All of it, however, had been demolished by the cannon. There were only stockades of great beams instead of a wall, and bundles of vine-branches, and jars full of earth. At that point a fierce battle ensued close in and with the weapons of hand-to-hand fighting. The heavy infantry and shield-bearers fought to overcome the defenders and get over the stockade, while the Romans and Italians tried to fight these off and to guard the stockade. At times the infantry did get over the wall and the stockade, pressing forward bravely and unhesitatingly. And at times they were stoutly forced back and driven off.

§ 220. The Sultan followed them up, as they struggled bravely, and encouraged them. He ordered those in charge of the cannon to put the match to the cannon. And these, being set off, fired their stone balls against the defenders and worked no little destruction on both sides, among those in the near vicinity.

§ 221. So, then, the two sides struggled and fought bravely and vigorously. Most of the night passed, and the Romans were successful and prevailed not a little. Also, Giustinianni and his men kept their positions stubbornly, and guarded the stockade and defended themselves bravely against the aggressors.

§ 222. And the other generals and officers with their own troops, and particularly the admiral of the fleet, also attacked the wall by land and sea and fought vigorously. The archers shot arrows from their bows, others fired cannon, and others brought up ladders and bridges and wooden towers and all sorts of machines to the walls. Some of them tried to climb up the wall by main force, especially where Zaganos and Karaja were in command.

§ 223. Zaganos had crossed the bridge in safety, and brought ladders and bridges up to the wall. He then tried to force the heavy infantry to climb up, leaving with him the archers and musketeers from the ships inside the harbor. These fired from the decks fiercely, attacking the left flank of those who were on the fortifications as the ships sailed by.

§ 224. Karaja crossed the moat and bravely attacked, attempting to get through inside the demolished wall.

§ 225. But the Romans on their part met them stubbornly and repulsed them brilliantly. They fought bravely and proved superior to the Ottomans in battle. Indeed they showed that they were heroes, for not a one of all the things that occurred could deter them: neither the hunger attacking them, nor sleeplessness, nor continuous and ceaseless fighting, nor wounds and slaughter, nor the death of relatives before their very eyes, nor any of the other fearful things could make them give in, or diminish their previous zeal and determination. They valiantly kept on resisting as before, through everything, until evil and pitiless fortune betrayed them.

§ 226. Sultan Mehmed saw that the attacking divisions were very much worn out by the battle and had not made any progress worth mentioning, and that the Romans and Italians were not only fighting stoutly but were prevailing in the battle. He was very indignant at this, considering that it ought not to be endured any longer. Immediately he brought up the divisions which he had been reserving for later on, men who were extremely well armed, daring and brave, and far in advance of the rest in experience and valor. They were the elite of the army: heavy infantry, bowmen, and lancers, and his own bodyguard, and along with them those of the division called Yenitsari [Janissaries].

§ 227. Calling to them and urging them to prove themselves now as heroes, he led the attack against the wall, himself at the head until they reached the moat. There he ordered the bowmen, slingers, and musketeers to stand at a distance and fire to the right, against the defenders on the palisade and on the battered wall. They were to keep up so heavy a fire that those defenders would be unable to fight, or to expose themselves because of the cloud of arrows and other projectiles falling like snowflakes.

§ 228. To all the rest, the heavy infantry and the shield-bearers, the Sultan gave orders to cross the moat swiftly and attack the palisade. With a loud and terrifying war-cry and with fierce impetuosity and wrath, they advanced as if mad. Being young and strong and full of daring, and especially because they were fighting in the Sultan's presence, their valor exceeded every expectation. They attacked the palisade and fought bravely without any hesitation. Needing no further orders, they knocked down the turrets which had been built out in front, broke the yardarms, scattered the materials that had been gathered, and forced the defenders back inside the palisade.

§ 229. Giustinianni with his men, and the Romans in that section fought bravely with lances, axes, pikes, javelins, and other weapons of offense. It was a hand-to-hand encounter, and they stopped the attackers and prevented them from getting inside the palisade. There was much shouting on both sides—the mingled sounds of blasphemy, insults, threats, attackers, defenders, shooters, those shot at, killers and dying, of those who in anger and wrath did all sorts of terrible things. And it was a sight to see there: a hard fight going on hand-to-hand with great determination and for the greatest rewards, heroes fighting valiantly, the one party struggling with all their might to force back the defenders, get possession of the wall, enter the City, and fall upon the children and women and the treasures, the other party bravely agonizing to drive them off and guard their possessions, even if they were not to succeed in prevailing and in keeping them.

§ 230. Instead, the hapless Romans were destined finally to be brought under the yoke of servitude and to suffer its horrors. For although they battled bravely, and though they lacked nothing of willingness and daring in the contest, Giustinianni received a mortal wound in the breast from an arrow fired by a crossbow. It passed clear through his breast-plate, and he fell where he was and was carried to his tent in a hopeless condition. All who were with him were scattered, being upset by their loss. They abandoned the palisade and wall where they had been fighting, and thought of only one thing—how they could carry him on to the galleons and get away safe themselves.

§ 231. But the Emperor Constantine besought them earnestly, and made promises to them if they would wait a little while, till the fighting should subside. They would not consent, however, but taking up their leader and all their armor, they boarded the galleons in haste and with all speed, giving no consideration to the other defenders.

§ 232. The Emperor Constantine forbade the others to follow. Then, though he had no idea what to do next—for he had no other reserves to fill the places thus left vacant, the ranks of those who had so suddenly deserted, and meantime the battle raged fiercely and all had to see to their own ranks and places and fight there—still, with his remaining Romans and his bodyguard, which was so few as to be easily counted, he took his stand in front of the palisade and fought bravely.

§ 233. Sultan Mehmed, who happened to be fighting quite near by, saw that the palisade and the other part of the wall that had been destroyed were now empty of men and deserted by the defenders. He noted that men were slipping away secretly and that those who remained were fighting feebly because they were so few. Realizing from this that the defenders had fled and that the wall was deserted, he shouted out: "Friends, we have the City! We have it! They are already fleeing from us! They can't stand it any longer! The wall is bare of defenders! It needs just a little more effort and the City is taken! Don't weaken, but on with the work with all your might, and be men and I am with you!"

Capture of the City

§ 234. So saying, he led them himself. And they, with a shout on the run and with a fearsome yell, went on ahead of the Sultan, pressing on up to the palisade. After a long and bitter struggle they hurled back the Romans from there and climbed by force up the palisade. They dashed some of their foe down into the ditch between the great wall and the palisade, which was deep and hard to get out of, and they killed them there. The rest they drove back to the gate.

Death of Emperor Constantine

§ 235. He had opened this gate in the great wall, so as to go easily over to the palisade. Now there was a great struggle there and great slaughter among those stationed there, for they were attacked by the heavy infantry and not a few others in irregular formation, who had been attracted from many points by the shouting. There the Emperor Constantine, with all who were with him, fell in gallant combat.

§ 236. The heavy infantry were already streaming through the little gate into the City, and others had rushed in through the breach in the great wall. Then all the rest of the army, with a rush and a roar, poured in brilliantly and scattered all over the City. And the Sultan stood before the great wall, where the standard also was and the ensigns, and watched the proceedings. The day was already breaking.

Great Rush, and Many Killed

§ 237. Then a great slaughter occurred of those who happened to be there: some of them were on the streets, for they had already left the houses and were running toward the tumult when they fell unexpectedly on the swords of the

71

soldiers; others were in their own homes and fell victims to the violence of the Janissaries and other soldiers, without any rhyme or reason; others were resisting, relying on their own courage; still others were fleeing to the churches and making supplication—men, women, and children, everyone, for there was no quarter given.

§ 238. The soldiers fell on them with anger and great wrath. For one thing, they were actuated by the hardships of the siege. For another, some foolish people had hurled taunts and curses at them from the battlements all through the siege. Now, in general they killed so as to frighten all the City, and to terrorize and enslave all by the slaughter.

Plunder of the City

§ 239. When they had had enough of murder, and the City was reduced to slavery, some of the troops turned to the mansions of the mighty, by bands and companies and divisions, for plunder and spoil. Others went to the robbing of churches, and others dispersed to the simple homes of the common people, stealing, robbing, plundering, killing, insulting, taking and enslaving men, women, and children, old and young, priests, monks—in short, every age and class.

Here, too, a Sad Tragedy

§ 240. There was a further sight, terrible and pitiful beyond all tragedies: young and chaste women of noble birth and well to do, accustomed to remain at home and who had hardly ever left their own premises, and handsome and lovely maidens of splendid and renowned families, till then unsullied by male eyes—some of these were dragged by force from their chambers and hauled off pitilessly and dishonorably.

§ 241. Other women, sleeping in their beds, had to endure nightmares. Men with swords, their hands bloodstained with murder, breathing out rage, speaking out murder indiscriminate, flushed with all the worst things—this crowd, made up of men from every race and nation, brought together by chance, like wild and ferocious beasts, leaped into the houses, driving them out mercilessly, dragging, rending, forcing, hauling them disgracefully into the public highways, insulting them and doing every evil thing.

§ 242. They say that many of the maidens, even at the mere unaccustomed sight and sound of these men, were terror-stricken and came near losing their very lives. And there were also honorable old men who were dragged by their white hair, and some of them beaten unmercifully. And well-born and beautiful young boys were carried off.

§ 243. There were priests who were driven along, and consecrated virgins who were honorable and wholly unsullied, devoted to God alone and living for Him to whom they had consecrated themselves. Some of these were forced out of their cells and driven off, and others dragged out of the churches where they had taken refuge and driven off with insult and dishonor, their cheeks scratched, amid wailing and lamentation and bitter tears. Tender children were snatched pitilessly from their mothers, young brides separated ruthlessly from their newly-married husbands. And ten thousand other terrible deeds were done.

Plundering and Robbing of the Churches

§ 244. And the desecrating and plundering and robbing of the churches—how can one describe it in words? Some things they threw in dishonor on the ground—ikons and reliquaries and other objects from the churches. The crowd snatched some of these, and some were given over to the fire while others were torn to shreds and scattered at the crossroads. The last resting-places of the blessed men of old were opened, and their remains were taken out and disgracefully torn to pieces, even to shreds, and made the sport of the wind while others were thrown on the streets.

§ 245. Chalices and goblets and vessels to hold the holy sacrifice, some of them were used for drinking and carousing, and others were broken up or melted down and sold. Holy vessels and costly robes richly embroidered with much gold or brilliant with precious stones and pearls were some of them given to the most wicked men for no good use, while others were consigned to the fire and melted down for the gold.

§ 246. And holy and divine books, and others mainly of profane literature and philosophy, were either given to the flames or dishonorably trampled under foot. Many of them were sold for two or three pieces of money, and sometimes for pennies only, not for gain so much as in contempt. Holy altars were torn from their foundations and overthrown. The walls of sanctuaries and cloisters were explored, and the holy places of the shrines were dug into and overthrown in the search for gold. Many other such things they dared to do.

§ 247. Those unfortunate Romans who had been assigned to other parts of the wall and were fighting there, on land and by the sea, supposed that the City was still safe and had not suffered reverses, and that their women and children were free—for they had no knowledge at all of what had happened. They kept on fighting lustily, powerfully resisting the attackers and brilliantly driving off those who were trying to scale the walls. But when they saw the enemy in their rear, attacking them from inside the City, and saw women and children being led away captives and shamefully treated, some were overwhelmed with hopelessness and threw themselves with their weapons over the wall and were killed, while others in utter despair dropped their weapons from hands already paralyzed, and surrendered to the enemy without a struggle, to be treated as the enemy chose.

Death of Orhan

§ 248. Orhan, the uncle of the Sultan, of the Ottoman family, happened to be present there at the time and fighting on the wall with them [the Byzantines], for the Emperor Constantine had him in the City and was treating him with much respect and honor because of his hopes. Orhan had been a fugitive for a long time through fear of his brother who had tried to kill him. When he saw that the City was captured, he sought to save himself. At first he thought he would run away secretly, as if he were one of the army, because of his uniform and of his correct pronunciation [of Greek]. But as soon as he saw he was recognized and being pursued, he threw himself immediately from the wall and died. And the soldiers rushed up, cut off his head, and took it to the Sultan, for he had wished to see him quickly, dead or alive.

§ 249. At this same time Hamza, Admiral of the fleet, when he saw the City already taken and the heavy infantry plundering it, quickly sailed up to the chain, cut it, and got inside the harbor. And of all the Roman ships which he found (for the Italian triremes and galleons had immediately put on all sail and made for the open sea), he sank some on the spot, and others he captured with all hands and ran them aground at what is called the Imperial Gate. When he found this still shut, he broke open the locks and bars and knocked down the gates.

§ 250. Entering the City with his marines, he found there many of the Romans gathered and making a brave stand. The [Ottoman] land forces had not yet reached that point, as they were plundering the rest of the City. Encountering these, he overcame them and killed them all, so that much blood flowed out of the gates. At that juncture the land army also arrived.

§ 251. In the same way, the sea army streamed in victoriously through the other shore gates, smashing them and throwing them down. Thus the whole naval force, scattering through the whole City, turned to plunder, robbing everything in their way, and falling on it like a fire or a whirlwind, burning and annihilating everything, or like a torrent sweeping away and destroying all things. For they hunted out everything, more carefully than Datis is said to have done in Eretria. Churches, holy places, old treasuries, tombs, underground galleries, cisterns and hiding-places, caves and crannies were burst into. And they searched every other hidden place, dragging out into the light anybody or anything they found hidden.

§ 252. Going into the largest church, that of the Holy Wisdom,[10] they found there a great crowd of men, women, and children taking refuge and calling upon God. Those

10 Sancta Sophia.

they caught as in a net, and took them all in a body and carried them captives, some to the galleys and some to the camp.

Surrender of Galata to the Sultan

§ 253. Upon this, the men of Galata, seeing the City already captured and plundered, immediately surrendered en masse to the Sultan so as to suffer no ills. They opened their gates to admit Zaganos and his troops, and these did them no harm.

§ 254. The entire army, the land force and the marine, poured into the City from daybreak and even from early dawn until the evening. They robbed and plundered it, carrying all the booty into the camp and into the ships. But some, like thieves, stole some of the booty and secretly went out of the gates and off to their abodes. Thus the whole City was emptied and deserted, despoiled and blackened as if by fire. One might easily disbelieve that it had ever had in it a human dwelling or the wealth or properties of a city or any furnishing or ornament of a household. And this was true although the City had been so magnificent and grand. There were left only ruined homes, so badly ruined as to cause great fear to all who saw them.

Number of Romans who died in the struggle, and of the prisoners taken

§ 255. There died, of Romans and of foreigners, as was reported, in all the fighting and in the capture itself, all told, men, women, and children, well-nigh four thousand, and a little more than fifty thousand were taken prisoners, including about five hundred from the whole army.

Entry of the Sultan into the City, and his seeing of it all, and his grief

§ 256. After this the Sultan entered the City and looked about to see its great size, its situation, its grandeur and beauty, its teeming population, its loveliness, and the costliness of its churches and public buildings and of the private houses and community houses and of those of the officials. He also saw the setting of the harbor and of the arsenals, and how skilfully and ingeniously they had everything arranged in the City—in a word, all the construction and adornment of it. When he saw what a large number had been killed, and the ruin of the buildings, and the wholesale ruin and destruction of the City, he was filled with compassion and repented not a little at the destruction and plundering. Tears fell from his eyes as he groaned deeply and passionately: "What a city we have given over to plunder and destruction!"

Sympathy

§ 257. Thus he suffered in spirit. And indeed this was a great blow to us, in this one city, a disaster the like of which had occurred in no one of the great renowned cities of history, whether one speaks of the size of the captured City or of the bitterness and harshness of the deed. And no less did it astound all others than it did those who went through it and suffered, through the unreasonable and unusual character of the event and through the overwhelming and unheard-of horror of it.

Comparison with other captures.
Comparison with that of Troy

§ 258. Troy was captured, but by Greeks and after ten years' fighting. Thus even if in point of the number of those killed and captured the disaster was not less or perhaps even greater, still both of these circumstances gave a certain relief and comfort to her. For the Greeks acted more philanthropically toward their prisoners, respecting their common Fates, while the prolonged and lengthy fighting and the daily expectation of capture had dulled the acuteness of feeling toward such sufferings. The present capture, however, was altogether devoid of any comfort.

Comparison with that of Babylon

§ 259. Babylon was captured by Cyrus, but it was given

no mortal wound nor was it enslaved by a captivity or given over to the dishonoring of women and children. It merely exchanged despots, getting a good one in place of a bad.

Comparison with that of Carthage

§ 260. Carthage was captured twice by Scipio. But the first time, by giving hostages and paying the costs of the war, it suffered simply a financial loss. And the second time, though forced to establish themselves a little farther away, with their women and children and all their belongings, and with their hostages restored safe and sound, they suffered no such horror.

Comparison with that of Rome

§ 261. Rome was captured, first by the Kelts and Gauls, and secondly by the Goths. But it suffered no such horror, but was simply tyrannized over for a time, and its economy and wealth impaired. The property of the first families was confiscated, and its illustrious men were exiled. And again, a little later, having recovered, she rose to a new height of glory and wealth and power and good fortune.

Comparison with that of Jerusalem

§ 262. Jerusalem was captured three times: by the Assyrians the first time, by Antiochus the second time, and by the Romans the third time. But the first time she sustained simply a transfer, with women and children and belongings, to Babylon. Under Antiochus, they were under a tyrant for a short time, and then again possessed their city. Under the Romans, even though the sufferings of the capture were insupportable, yet there had been in the city many terrible uprisings of a civil nature, with plunderings and slaughters and merciless murders of the inhabitants and even of members of their own families, both before and during that last war. Many times people had prayed fervently that the city might be captured so that they might thus find relief from those terrible evils, either in death or in slavery.

Comparison with Other Cities

§ 263. Therefore the fall of those other cities cannot be compared with that of this City. Still other cities, many and large, in Asia and Europe, have been captured. They were flourishing in wealth, glory, learning, the valor of their inhabitants, and in many other worthy aspects. But the sufferings of these cities were not comparable to the present horrors.

Comparison of this City with itself, that is, with the capture by the Latins and . . . alas!

§ 264. This hapless City was also captured by the Western peoples, tyrannized over for sixty years,[11] and robbed of great wealth and of many very beautiful and costly statues from the churches. The brilliant and honored and sought-after masterpieces which had been seen and heard of by all were carried off to the west, while those which were left in the City became the prey of the flames. But loss and suffering were limited to that, though of course that alone was no small thing. Of the inhabitants, however, no one lost wife or children or was deprived of his most valuable things. All the inhabitants were unharmed and unmolested. Then, having overthrown the tyranny and recovered herself, the City regained its former state and was a seat of empire again, ruling over many races in Asia and Europe and not a few islands. It became splendid and rich and glorious and famed, a ruler and an example in all good things, the center of learning and culture and wisdom and virtue, in fact, of all the best things in one.

Personal Lamentation and Soliloquy over the City

§ 265. But this time the City's possessions vanished, its goods summarily disappeared, and it was deprived of all things: wealth, glory, rule, splendor, honor, brilliance of population, valor, education, wisdom, religious orders, domin-

11 The "Fourth Crusade" and the Latin rule of Constantinople, 1204-1261.

ion—in short, of all. And in the degree in which the City had advanced in prosperity and good fortune, to a corresponding degree it was now brought down into the abyss of misfortune and misery.

§ 266. While previously it had been called blessed by very many, it now heard everyone call it unfortunate and deeply afflicted. And while it had gloriously advanced to the boundaries of the civilized world, it now filled land and sea alike with its misfortunes and its ignominy, sending everywhere as examples of its misery the inhabitants, men, women, and children, who were scattered disgracefully in captivity and slavery and insult.

§ 267. And the City which had formerly ruled with honor and glory and wealth and great splendor over many nations was now ruled by others, amid want and disgrace and dishonor and abject and shameful slavery.

§ 268. While it had been an example of all good things, the picture of brilliant prosperity, it now became the picture of misfortune, a reminder of sufferings, a monument of disaster, and a by-word for life.

Soliloquy on the uncertainty of human affairs and the mutability of present things, and how nothing is lasting or certain

§ 269. So there is in human affairs nothing trustworthy or sure, but everything is like the Euripus, twisting and turning up and down, in turn playing with and being played with by the fickle changes of life. And it will never cease from this irregular and noisy ebb and flow, or the coming and going of one against another, as long as things are as they are.

§ 270. But the thing I wonder at the rather is this: the parallelism of names occurring in the changed circumstances, while the City went on for such a long period, or for nearly 1200 years. For Constantine, the fortunate Emperor, son of Helen, built her and brought her to the pitch of happiness and fortune. And now again, under Constantine, the unfortunate Emperor, son of Helen, she is taken and reduced to the worst slavery and misfortune.

§ 271. The thirty triremes that the High Priest of Rome had sent as a help to the City and to Constantine, reached Chios where they met with adverse winds and remained, awaiting suitable weather. But after a short time they heard of the capture of the City. So, as their help was too late, they sailed for home again, having accomplished nothing that they started out to do. It was fated that this unfortunate City should inevitably be captured and suffer. Therefore it had to be deprived of all succor from any possible quarter which might have helped it, for so had God decreed.

Date of Capture

§ 272. Thus, then, it was captured from the Romans under the Emperor Constantine, seventh of the Palaeologi, on the 29th of May in the 6961st year from the beginning [A.D. 1453] and 1124 years after the founding and establishment of the City.

Elegy over Emperor Constantine

§ 273. The Emperor Constantine himself, as I said, died fighting. He was wise and moderate in his private life and diligent to the highest degree in prudence and virtue, sagacious as the most highly-trained of men. In political affairs and in matters of government he yielded to no one of the kings before him in preeminence. Quick to perceive his duty, and still more quick to do it, he was eloquent in speech, clever in thought, and very accomplished in talking of public affairs.

§ 274. He was exact in his judgments of the present, as someone has said of Pericles, and usually correct in regard to the future, a splendid worker, who chose to do and to suffer everything for the fatherland and for his subjects. Therefore, when he saw with his own eyes the evident danger threatening the City, and was able to save himself, he did not choose to do so, although there were many who begged him to, but preferred to die with his country and his subjects, or rather to die beforehand himself, so that he might not see his country captured and all the inhabitants either cruelly murdered or made captive and ignominiously taken away.

§ 275. For when he saw the enemy pressing in on him and coming into the City through the broken wall, he is stated to have cried aloud this last word: "The city is taken and it is useless for me to live any longer." So saying he hurled himself into the midst of the enemy and was cut to pieces. He was a splendid man and the guardian of the common good, but unfortunate all through his life and doubly unfortunate at its close.

Epilogue

§ 276. As for the great City of Constantine, raised to a great height of glory and dominion and wealth in its own times, overshadowing to an infinite degree all the cities around it, renowned for its glory, wealth, authority, power, and greatness, and all its other qualities, it thus came to its end.

§ 277. The Sultan Mehmed, when he had carefully viewed the City and all its contents, went back to the camp and divided the spoils. First he took the customary toll of the spoils for himself. Then also, as prizes from all the rest, he chose out beautiful virgins and those of the best families, and the handsomest boys, some of whom he even bought from the soldiers. He also chose some of the distinguished men who, he was informed, were above the rest in family and intelligence and valor. Among these was Notaras himself, a man among the most able and notable in knowledge, wealth, virtue, and political power. The Sultan honored him with a personal interview, spoke soothing words to him, and filled him with hope, and not him only but the rest who were with him.

§ 278. For the Sultan was overcome with pity for the men and their misfortune, as he saw from what good circumstances they had fallen into such great predicaments. And he had good intentions towards them, even though his ill will soon overcame these plans.

§ 279. After arranging these affairs and all that concerned with the soldiers, suitably in accordance with his intentions, he honored some of them with government positions and offices, and others with money, and still others with stipends and many other sorts of gifts. He also did kindnesses to and personally received those whom he knew to have fought well. And after making an address to them and telling them many things, praising and thanking them, he disbanded the army.

§ 280. Then, with the notable men, and his courtiers, he went through the City. First he planned how to repopulate it, not merely as it formerly was but more completely, if possible, so that it should be a worthy capital for him, situated, as it was, most favorably by land and by sea. Then he donated to all the grandees, and to those of his household, the magnificent homes of the rich, with gardens and fields and vineyards inside of the City. And to some of them he even gave beautiful churches as their private residences.

§ 281. For himself, he chose the most beautiful location in the center of the City for the erection of a royal palace. After this, he settled all the captives whom he had taken as his portion, together with their wives and children, along the shores of the city harbor, since they were sea-faring men whom they previously had called Stenites. He gave them houses and freed them from taxes for a specified time.

§ 282. He also made a proclamation to all those who had paid their own ransom, or who promised to pay it to their masters within a limited time, that they might live in the City, and he granted them, also, freedom from taxes, and gave them houses, either their own or those of others.

§ 283. He wanted those of the nobility whom he approved of to live there with their wives and children. Accordingly he gave them houses and lands and provisions for living, and tried in every way to help them. This was his intention and purpose, as has been stated.

§ 284. He contemplated making Notaras the commandant of the City, and putting him in charge of its repopulation, and he had advised with him previously regarding this. But the arrows of envy laid that man and his sons low with mortal wounds, and they were condemned to an unjust death.

Advice of those in high position to the King
to remove the men. The fate of the family

§ 285. For some men of great influence, I know not
whence, moved by envy and hatred toward those men, persuaded him, since he had them in his power, to put them out
of the way, saying that Romans, and especially prominent
ones, not only ought not to live in this City or occupy any
positions but even should not live at all, or go about the
place. For, they said, after recuperating a little and having
become free from slavery, those men would no longer hesitate
to plot in their own interests and seek to get back what they
formerly had, and especially their freedom. Thus they would
do all they could against the City, or else would desert to
our enemies, even while remaining here. Persuaded by these
arguments, or rather being dissuaded from his intention, the
Sultan ordered the men to be removed. And they were all
killed, and among them were executed the Grand Duke and
his two sons.

§ 286. They say that when this man was taken to the
place of execution, he begged the executioner first to kill his
children before his very eyes, so that in terror at his death
they might not abjure their faith. And so, as he waited to
be sacrificed with his children, he watched attentively while
his sons were being executed, without turning his eyes, and
unterrified in mind. Then, after praying and thanking God
for taking home his children and himself, he bared his neck
to the sword. Thus bravely and with firm and lofty sentiments, he died with the spirit of a hero.

An Estimate of the Grand Duke

§ 287. This man was devout in all relations with God,
and of signal prudence, known for the loftiness of his sentiments and the sharpness of his intellect and the freedom of
his spirit from all trammels. Through it all he exhibited both
physical and moral greatness. Through these he attained
political reputation, secured power in public affairs, and attained great glory and wealth. He was in the front rank in the

estimation not only of the Romans but also of many from other nations. And his companions, nine in number, died bravely, with steady and manly courage.

§ 288. Later on, the Sultan discovered the underhandedness and wickedness of those who had persuaded him to put these men to death, and in disgust at their treachery he removed them from his sight, condemning some of them to death, and depriving the rest of their positions and honors. Thus they were not long in paying the penalty for their injustice to these men. But all this we shall refer to a little later.

Arrival of Embassies to the Sultan at Adrianople

§ 289. Then he appointed as regent of the City and its suburbs a most intelligent and useful man, possessed of the finest manners, Suleiman by name. He put him in charge of everything, but in particular over the repopulating of the City, and instructed him to be very zealous about this matter. Having done this, the Sultan went back to Adrianople at harvest time.

§ 290. There he received delegations from the Triballians [Serbs], and Illyrians [Albanians], and Peloponnesians, also from the people of Mitylene and Chios, and many others. To all of these he acted graciously. With some he made a truce and gave and received pledges. To others he granted what they asked. To some he remitted taxes, and to others he performed some other kindness, and to all he spoke peaceably.

§ 291. Similarly he gave audience to ambassadors sent him from the rulers of Persia and of Egypt, and also from Karaman, prince of the Cilicians, who all congratulated him on his accomplishments and praised him for his valor and virtue and zeal for his nation. These he received gladly, and honored with rich and varied and numerous gifts, including some of the spoils. And he sent them away with great ceremony.

§ 292. After this he appointed some of the youths of high family, whom he had chosen according to their merits, to be in his bodyguard and to be constantly near him, and others to other service as his pages. He admired them for their prudence and other virtues and for their training. They were indeed of signal physical beauty and nobility and talent of soul, and in their manners and morals they were outstanding, for they were of high and renowned ancestry and splendid physique, and well trained in the royal palace.

§ 293. So, too, he admired the modesty, grace, and beauty of the virgins, and their superiority among their race in every sort of good trait.

Arrival of Ambassadors whom Kritovoulos sent to surrender the islands of Thasos, Imbros, and Lemnos

§ 294. During those days there arrived also the embassy from the islands to the Sultan, which Kritovoulos the Imbriote, the author of this book, had sent. They were to give over to him the islands in the Aegean Sea, Imbros, Lemnos, and Thasos, which had formerly been subject to the Emperor Constantine. But the chiefs sent by him in these delegations, on first hearing of the capture of the City and the death of the Emperor, had taken flight, despairing of everything.

§ 295. Those from Lemnos went off with the Italian triremes escaping from the City, which had touched at the point of Lemnos on their return to their homes. Those from Imbros had sailed with the heavy transports to the cape called Cephalos, in Imbros, and the people of the islands, seeing the flight of their chiefs, were terrified at a possible attack by the Sultan's fleet, if it should sail against them. For they had learned that the fleet had already returned to Gallipoli. Therefore they resolved to flee.

§ 296. In fact, nearly two hundred men of the Lemniotes, with their wives and children, did flee, some to Crete, some to Chios, and some to Euboea.

§ 297. Learning this, Kritovoulos halted their impetuosity, encouraged them with well-founded hopes, and secretly sent a trustworthy man to Hamza, Governor of Gallipoli and Admiral of the entire fleet, and made an agreement with him not to sail against the islands, nor do them any harm at all, nor even plan it. He persuaded him by sending him many gifts. Through the Admiral he also sent ambassadors to the Sultan—the priest of the island, and with him the chief man of the inhabitants. These men brought gifts and surrendered the islands to him, at the same time begging him to allow the inhabitants to remain as before, and promising to pay over to him whatever taxes he levied, year by year, and to receive as governor whomever he appointed.

The Islands given over by the Sultan to the rulers of Enos and Mitylene, Palamedes and Dorieus

§ 298. The Sultan received these men kindly, granted their requests, and entrusted the islands as follows, in accordance with the arrangement made in the time of the Emperor: namely, Imbros to Palamedes, governor of Enos, and Lemnos and Thasos to Dorieus, chief of Mitylene. It so happened that the latter, Dorieus, had sent his elder son to the Sultan, and the former, Palamedes, had sent one of his highest officials, a very near relative, to ask for these very islands. The messengers sent by Kritovoulos, being entrusted with a similar task, themselves also made the same request from the Sultan. Thus the islands were freed from danger for the time, for no small danger had threatened them through the return of the fleet from the City to Gallipoli.

Arrest and execution of Halil

§ 299. During this same period the Sultan arrested Halil also, one of his first-rank men and very powerful, and put him in prison. And after torturing him in many ways, he put him to death. In his possession was found much silver and gold money and every sort of wealth, collected during many years both by his ancestors and by himself. For he belonged to one of the first families among them, renowned for glory, wealth, and power. All this wealth the Sultan turned into the royal treasury, except for a very limited sum which he allotted to the sons. Later on, however, he gave it all back to these sons.

§ 300. The Sultan had ample reasons to be angry with Halil. Chief of these were the following: While the Sultan's father was still reigning, Halil had worked against Mehmed in many ways and had been a strong force against him. And when the father had once appointed Mehmed lord of the whole realm, then on the advice of Halil he subsequently revoked this appointment. Also during Mehmed's campaign against the City, Halil had tried to dissuade the Sultan from it. Further, he had had secret negotiations with the Romans, trying to make the Sultan's efforts miscarry. In every way he worked against the Sultan and opposed him. These were the openly avowed reasons for his arrest and execution, but there were also other secret ones.

Ishak brought into the place and power of Halil

§ 301. In place of this man, the Sultan substituted Ishak, a man of the wisest sort, experienced in many spheres but especially a military leader and a man of courage.

§ 302. After a few days, he also dismissed Zaganos, and deprived him of rule and rank. He also put away the daughter of Zaganos, whom he had recently married, and sent father and daughter back into Asia, granting them there a piece of land large enough to support them.

§ 303. The Sultan substituted for him in his position in general oversight, his kinsman by marriage with Zaganos's other daughter, a man named Mahmud, who had formerly belonged to the Roman nation on both his father's and his mother's side. His paternal grandfather, Philaninos, had been ruler of Hellas, with the rank of Caesar. This man had so fine a nature that he outshone not only all his contemporaries but also his predecessors in wisdom, bravery, virtue, and other good qualities. He was very quick to recognize spontaneously what needed to be done, even when another told him of it, and still quicker in carrying it out. He was also eloquent in addressing a crowd, able in commanding men, and still more clever in making use of things and in finding a way out of difficulties. He was enterprising, a good counsellor, bold, courageous, excelling in all lines, as the times and circumstances proved him to be.

§ 304. For from the time he took charge of the affairs of the great Sultan, he gave everything in this great dominion a better prospect by his wonderful zeal and his fine planning as well as by his implicit and unqualified faith in and goodwill towards his sovereign. He was thus a man of better character than them all, as shown by his accomplishments.

§ 305. When the Sultan had done these things in Adrianople, he went back in .the autumn to Byzantium, so the year 6961 counting from the beginning went by, which was the third of the Sultan's reign [A.D. 1453].

PART II

SUMMARY

This includes the history of the expedition into Enos, the fight with the Triballi and their total defeat and enslavement, and the capture of the islands of Lemnos, Thasos, and Samothrace by the Italians. Time involved: four years [A.D. 1454-1457].

Repopulating of the City

§ 1. When the Sultan had captured the City of Constantine, almost his very first care was to have the City repopulated. He also undertook the further care and repairs of it. He sent an order in the form of an imperial command to every part of his realm, that as many inhabitants as possible be transferred to the City, not only Christians but also his own people and many of the Hebrews.

Repair of the walls thrown down by the cannon, as well as of the other land-walls and sea-walls; the building of the Palace, and the building of the fortress at the Golden Gate

§ 2. Next he ordered that those parts of the wall which had been destroyed by the cannon should all be strongly rebuilt, and that wherever else they had been damaged by the ravages of time, along the land or along the sea, they should be repaired. He also laid the foundations of the royal palace, choosing, as I said, the finest and best location in the City. He further ordered the construction of a strong fortress near the Golden Gate where there had formerly been an imperial castle, and he commanded that all these things should be done with all haste.

§ 3. He commanded also that the Roman prisoners should work, and should receive a daily wage of six aspers or more. This was in a way a piece of wise foresight on the part of the Sultan, for it fed the prisoners and enabled them to provide for their own ransom by earning enough to pay their masters thus. Also, when they should become free, they might dwell in the City. Not only this, but it also showed great philanthropy and beneficence, and proved the magnanimity of the Sultan.

§ 4. In fact, he dealt in this fashion with everybody, and not least with these prisoners. He took pity on them, and every day would do some good turn with enthusiasm. Often when he left the palace and went about the City, to see the sights or for any other reason, if he ran across such persons anywhere, he would at once draw up his horse and distribute freely to all, with his own hand, silver coins and often gold ones. Such mercy he had for men.

The Calling of Gennadius; his appointment as Patriarch

§ 5. During that period he called back Gennadius, a very wise and remarkable man. He had already heard much through common report about the wisdom and prudence and virtue of this man. Therefore, immediately after the capture he sought for him, being anxious to see him and to hear some of his wisdom. And after a painstaking search he found him at Adrianople in a village, kept under guard in the home of one of the notables, but enjoying great honors. For his captor knew of his virtue, even though he himself was a military man.

§ 6. When the Sultan saw him, and had in a short time had proofs of his wisdom and prudence and virtue and also of his power as a speaker and of his religious character, he was greatly impressed with him, and held him in great honor and respect, and gave him the right to come to him at any time, and honored him with liberty and conversation. He enjoyed his various talks with him and his replies, and he loaded him with noble and costly gifts.

§ 7. In the end, he made him Patriarch and High Priest of the Christians, and gave him among many other rights and privileges the rule of the church and all its power and authority, no less than that enjoyed previously under the emperors. He also granted him the privilege of delivering before him fearlessly and freely many good disquisitions concerning the Christian faith and doctrine. And he himself went to his residence, taking with him the dignitaries and wise men of his court, and thus paid him great honor. And in many other ways he delighted the man.

§ 8. Thus the Sultan showed that he knew how to respect

the true worth of any man, not only of military men but of every class, kings, and tyrants, and emperors. Furthermore the Sultan gave back the church to the Christians, by the will of God, together with a large portion of its properties.

The Sultan crosses into Asia, and arranges affairs there

§ 9. Having thus settled affairs in the City, the Sultan crossed over into Asia. When he arrived in Bursa he paid honors to his father, holding a religious and memorial service at his tomb with all magnificence and adorning the mausoleum with costly offerings and royal gifts.

§ 10. Then he put in good order all the affairs in Asia, regulating all that had to do with local disturbances, revolts of leaders and peoples, and all else.

§ 11. Further, he removed men from positions in provinces and sub-provinces, and placed there new governors and sub-governors, and put in very good order everything in that region according to his best judgment, and all in the space of thirty-five days.

Arrival of the Sultan at Adrianople, and the despatch of the fleet under Yunus to the islands near Rhodes and Naxos

§ 12. He appointed Hamza as Commander in Chief of all Asia, and immediately returned to Byzantium. There he remained only a short time, just long enough to examine the buildings that had been constructed there, and give orders about further work on them and on others, stipulating that it be done as quickly as possible. And then he set out for Adrianople in the winter.

§ 13. When he arrived there, he immediately sent for Yunus, governor of Gallipoli and admiral of the fleet, and ordered him to get the fleet fitted out with all speed and to sail to Naxos and the islands near Rhodes, Paros, Rhenaea, and Cos and the others in that vicinity.

§ 14. For when all the other islanders became vassals of

he Sultan the Rhodians alone would not accept the agreenents and the treaties offered by him, but refrained from illiances. And they accepted the services of the pirate ships)f the lower [or western] Iberians and Alanians[12] and hired)ther ships too, and ravaged all the coastlands of the Sultan. io also the men of Naxos connived at the incursions of the)irates, and furnished them wheat and other needed supplies. Thus they did no little injury to the Sultan's domains.

Expedition of Yunus

§ 15. Therefore he sent his fleet against these people. Yunus equipped and armed eighty warships besides quite a few cargo ships and other ships carrying cannon. He then set sail from Gallipoli and went out through the straits of the Hellespont, right past Aegospotami, and going by Sestos and Abydos and the so-called Dog's Heads [Cynoscephalæ] ie reached Dardania, near the mouth of the Straits.

§ 16. Sailing by the river of Troy and the monument)f Achilles, he arrived at Tenedos. There he stayed two days ind took on water. He also collected all his ships, for some)f them were delayed, having stopped along the coasts of that region to collect rowers. He then weighed anchor by night, so as not to excite suspicions by being seen—for he wanted to escape observation as far as possible—and sailed into the Aegean Sea, having the Cyanid Islands astern on the right and Lesbos at the bow on his left.

Of a terrible storm, and the danger of the ships

§ 17. Suddenly a terrible storm broke on them, a tempest with torrents of rain, and lightning and thunder and raging winds and darkness. The sea grew wild, and a great hurricane arose, as frequently happens in the Aegean. At first the ships all sailed near the signal-beacon of the commander's ship, following her even through the night and the thick darkness. But, borne along by the fierce storm and hurricane and the irregularly shifting winds, they fell foul of each other and collided, and several of them sank.

12 Spanish or Catalan corsairs.

§ 18. In this way they came very near sinking the admiral's flagship, all of them falling foul of it at once, had not the captain, seeing the danger, quickly snuffed out the signal-beacon. Thus the ships were scattered here and there over the sea and were driven all night, battling with the storm until daylight, as each succeeded in saving itself from the billows.

§ 19. Some of them were carried away and sank at a short distance from the shore, impaled on the reefs and sunken rocks. The ships carrying the cannon were borne along irregularly by the force of the current and the winds, and were some of them dashed against the rocks of the coast and the cannon sank right there, while others were saved with difficulty at a late hour.

§ 20. Yunus, with six ships left him, after being buffeted and tossed about on the sea all day, barely managed to make the harbor in the island of Chios toward evening, soaked through, and having lost overboard everything that was on the decks. Through such great danger he had passed. Then, after a three days' stay in Chios, having gathered all the remainder of the fleet and laid in such supplies as were obtainable, he set sail from there and reached the island of Cos.

§ 21. Here he landed, and devastated the land of the Cosites. He also attacked the city and besieged it three days. But as he made no progress, he burned the houses outside of the city, overran all the rest of the island, sacked the villages and carried off much booty, which he placed in his ships, and sailed away.

Submission of Phocaea to Yunus

§ 22. Then he went against Phocaea, called the New, which belonged to the Chiotes, made a landing, and took possession of it by agreement. This he did in spite of the treaties, because he was angry with the Chiotes for not having received him well when he was driven there by the storm, and for not having honored him with suitable gifts.

§ 23. So, having arranged things in Phocaea according to his will, he left a garrison there, and took away some of the youth and sailed back home to Gallipoli. There he dismissed the fleet.

Yunus lost 25 ships in the storm

§ 24. He lost twenty-five of his ships in the storm, including all of the cargo ships. For this reason most of all, it is said, the Sultan was angry with him. For this cause, among others, soon after that he had Yunus executed.

Reasons why the Sultan made an expedition against the Triballi [Serbs]

§ 25. While the Sultan was spending the winter at Adrianople, he prepared a large expedition against the Triballi, for he had learned that there was a plot among them against him. The leader of the Triballi wished to start a revolt, and secretly sent word to the king of the Paeonians [Hungarians] and made a pact with him, so that he might make full preparation and cross the Ister [Danube] and attack the Sultan's domains at the same time that the other should attack.

§ 26. Not only that, but he also paid the customary tribute very late, and then only in part, always inventing excuses for his unjustifiable delays. The Sultan was all the more angered by this, because he saw proof in it that the man was plotting an intrigue.

The position of the land of the Triballi

§ 27. These things were not the only incitements to him. The nature of that country also gave him a convenient point for making war on the Paeonians and the Dacians,[13] who had made expeditions against him; and he could very easily attack their country from that of the Triballi. For the latter has a favorable position in Europe, beginning from the upper part of Mysia[14] and Mount Haemon [the Balkans], and reaching to the Ister River, which separates it from the territory of the Dacians and Paeonians.

[13] In modern Rumania.
[14] Or Moesia, the region between the Balkan range and the Danube.

Notes on the Ister

§ 28. The Ister, largest river in Europe, rises in the Keltic Mountains and, flowing through them and through the country of the Paeonians and Dacians and that of not a few other nations, traversing a great extent of land, and always increasing in size by the addition of inflowing streams, it ends by flowing through the Getian and Scythian country into the Euxine Sea.

§ 29. It embraces in its basin many other very warlike nations, but especially the Paeonians and Dacians, to whom, as I have said, the country of the Triballi is contiguous. The land stretches alongside these for a long distance, and contains many fine cities in the interior, with strong fortresses near the banks of the river. For this reason the Sultan deemed it necessary to seize the country and to get possession of the fortresses on the river-banks so as to become master of the crossings of the river and thus be able to cross into their country whenever he wished, and to prevent them from crossing into his.

Remarks on the land of the Triballi, its great fruitfulness and self-sufficiency in all things

§ 30. Not only this, but the fertility of the land had no small influence with him, as it was remarkably productive of all sorts of good things. For the earth is very fertile, and able to bear all crops. It produces everything in abundance, all sorts of grains and plants. Also whatever is raised on the earth, that is to say, flocks of goats and sheep, swine, cattle, and fine horses in no small quantity, as well as many other edible and useful animals of various kinds, both domesticated and wild, are produced in great numbers, together with much fodder for them.

§ 31. Its greatest asset, in which it surpasses all other lands, is that it produces gold and silver as if from springs. They are mined all over this region, which has many very fine deposits of both gold and silver, better than those of India. Indeed, the country of the Triballi has in this respect been fortunate from the start, and has prided itself on its wealth and power. It was a kingdom with many large cities in it, flourishing ones, and strong and impregnable castles. And it was rich in its supply of soldiers and armies, and of much good equipment.

§ 32. It had also inhabitants of the finest sort, and it nourished many youths of manly vigor. It was admired and renowned, nay, and envied, too, so that there were not simply many who loved it, but also those who plotted against it.

Relating how the country of the Triballi had formerly been captured by Sultan Murad

§ 33. Murad, the father of the Sultan, had previously campaigned against the country with a large powerful force which conquered the whole land and captured the cities and fortresses, both those inland and those situated on the banks of the Ister River. Some of these he took by assault, by force of arms, while others surrendered without a battle. Thus he held the whole country, having driven out into Paeonia Lazarus, the ruler of the land.[15]

§ 34. Now, when some time had passed since this conquest, the Sultan took pity on the conquered, both because of his nature and because he was begged by friends to do so, for he was as kindhearted as any man, in thought and action. Besides, the Sultan wanted this man as an ally and co-worker. The man had already become his friend, and had the highest sentiments as to the war against the Paeonians and Dacians, for he had long been their neighbor and knew their country and their customs well. Besides this, he was in every way a brave man and a warrior. So the Sultan gave him back his country and his rule, nor did he deprive him of anything which he had taken. Nay, rather, he gave him in addition many of his own things. He did not take a single hostage from him, but accepted only the customary taxes, bound him by oaths, and entrusted the rule to him.

§ 35. And Lazarus, having again undertaken to rule his country, became strong in a short time, and ruled it powerfully. He was submissive to the Sultan's father, and for a

---

[15] George Brankovich of the Lazarevich line.

while to Sultan Mehmed himself, and paid the tribute. But after that, as I have related, he became rash and determined to revolt. Nor did he willingly pay the tribute, but also co-operated with the Paeonians [Hungarians] and Dacians, thus breaking the treaties he had made with the Sultan.

Expedition of the Sultan against the Triballi

§ 36. When the Sultan discovered that he was acting in this way, he made an expedition against him. Having made careful preparations through the winter, at the very first appearance of spring he left Adrianople with all his army, both cavalry and infantry, and marched through the interior of Thrace and Macedonia, taking with him not a few cannon and weapons of all sorts.

As to the size of the army

§ 37. He had an army, it is stated, of 50,000 horse, and of footsoldiers a much larger number. Having reached Moesia and Mount Haemon (where was the pass) in a week, he crossed this safely with all his army, and in three days' march from here he entered the territory of the Triballi.

The Sultan's invasion of the land of the Triballi; attack and capture of castles

§ 38. He invaded and pillaged a large part of it, and he captured not a few fortresses, some by force and assault, others by siege. He did this in the space of twenty-five days from his first incursion. Then he came to a town well fortified and flourishing, Novoprodo [Novobrdo] as it was called in the language of the Triballi, where most of the silver and gold are mined.

Siege of Novoprodo

§ 39. He pitched his camp before this town. First he sent a message to the inhabitants, proposing their surrender and the making of a treaty, if they were willing, and stating that they should give over to him their city and themselves, with promises of good faith, and that they and their wives and children and all their goods should remain there safe and unhurt, in the same condition and footing as hitherto. He also required that they should pay him exactly the same taxes they had been giving to their own king, and that they should live peaceably with everybody else.

§ 40. But this attempt did not succeed as he had hoped, since the besieged were absolutely unwilling to accept. Therefore he immediately devastated the countryside, surrounded the town and besieged it with his army, and brought his cannon into action.

§ 41. Lazarus, the chief of the Triballi, when he heard of the great attack by the Sultan, of the capture of the fortresses and of the siege of Novoprodo, was astounded at what had occurred and altogether perplexed and embarrassed as to what to do.

§ 42. However, he did the best he could to put the remaining fortresses in condition, and he removed the men, women and children from the plains into the fortresses or else into mountain strongholds. The flocks he carried away, as also all the other possessions of the people, and he fortified the rest of the country.

Lazarus crosses into Dacia and stays there

§ 43. When he had placed a considerable garrison in Semendria with a commander who was one of those most trusted by him, and when he had brought to that place abundant supplies which he considered sufficient for a long siege, he himself crossed the Ister with his wife and children and all his goods, and with some of his suite.

Embassy from Lazarus to the Sultan, and the Treaty of the Sultan with him

§ 44. Reaching the country of the Dacians and Paeonians, he remained there. After a short time he thought it wise to send an embassy to the Sultan and to try, if possible, to secure in some way a treaty of peace. So he chose men of the highest rank around him, men of wisdom and education, and gave them many costly presents of gold and silver as well as the customary taxes which he owed, and sent them off.

§ 45. When they arrived, they brought the presents to the Sultan, and also the taxes, and gave him the message they had from their chief. The Sultan received them graciously and dealt kindly with them. He spoke peaceably to them, and made a treaty and gave and received pledges by which he was to keep only the fortresses he had captured and the territory he had taken by force of arms, while over all the remainder their chief was to rule, paying a yearly tribute somewhat less than formerly. The latter was also to furnish a stipulated number of soldiers for the expeditions of the Sultan.

Surrender of Novoprodo to the Sultan

§ 46. Now the besieged town of Novoprodo, unable to resist any longer the siege which had lasted a long time—for some forty days of siege had dragged on, and the walls had been demolished by the cannon—had already surrendered of its own accord to the Sultan, with the stipulation that all the inhabitants should be spared, and should stay as they were, with their wives and children and all their belongings, living in the town and tilling the land.

§ 47. Hence the Sultan, having made the treaty and exchanged pledges, honored the ambassadors with friendly and suitable gifts, saluted them with gracious and affable words, and sent them back. On their return they told their chief Lazarus what they had done.

§ 48. He had indeed succeeded beyond his expectations in getting the treaty (which he never could have hoped for), for he had not imagined it possible for the Sultan to make a treaty with him after he had raised such an army and made such great and expensive preparations for war. Therefore he was greatly pleased at the outcome, and did not care about anything he had lost, so happy was he at what remained. He had, indeed, expected to lose everything at once.

Return of Lazarus to his own country

§ 49. Therefore Lazarus immediately took his wife and hildren and all his other belongings, and crossed the Ister nd went to his own domain.

§ 50. As for the Sultan, when he had put the fortresses which he had captured in very safe condition, and when he iad placed a sufficient garrison in the country, he left as ;overnor Ali, a warrior and a nobleman. With a very large |uantity of booty for himself and his army, Sultan Mehmed hen went back to Adrianople.

§ 51. The summer was now ending. He stayed in Adrinople a short time. Then, leaving a member of his own suite n charge there, he went to Byzantium in the middle of the utumn, to spend the winter there. So closed the year 6963 1455] from the beginning, the fifth of the reign of the iultan.

How the Sultan took care of the City

§ 52. On reaching the City, he found the palace brilliantly :ompleted, and the castle at the Golden Gate and all the walls of the City well built. He was pleased at what had been done, and rewarded the overseers of the work with money and robes of ceremony and many other things. He also ordered them to repair as soon as possible the bridges over the gulfs of Athyras and Rhegium, which had been damaged in recent storms and had fallen. In addition, they were to repair and level the other roads that led to the City, wherever hey were dangerous or difficult to pass, by paving them with ilabs and stones so that travel on them should be easy and iafe.

§ 53. Not only this, but he ordered them to build caravaniaries and halting-places along the roads so that any travelers :oming by land toward the city might pass the night there ind rest.

§ 54. And he commanded them to construct a very large ind very fine marketplace, in the center of the City, somewhere near the palace, protected by very strong walls on the utside, and divided on the inside into very beautiful and spacious colonnades. It was to have a roof of fired tile and to be ornamented with dressed stone.

§ 55. He also ordered them to construct splendid and costly baths, and through aqueducts to bring into the City from the countryside an abundance of water. Many other such things he also ordered to be done for the building up and beautifying of the City, and for the benefit and needs and comfort of the inhabitants.

§ 56. Above all he was solicitous to work for the re-peopling of the City and to fill it with inhabitants as it had previously been. He gathered them there from all parts of Asia and Europe, and he transferred them with all possible care and speed, people of all nations, but more especially of Christians. So profound was the passion that came into his soul for the City and its peopling, and for bringing it back to its former prosperity.

Reasons why the Sultan invaded Enos

§ 57. While he was busy with these things, in the middle of winter, news came that Dorieus,[16] ruler of Enos and of the islands Imbros and Samothrace, wanted a change of government and was planning a revolution. This man's father, Palamedes, who had died a short time before, had named in his will Dorieus himself and the widow of the latter's elder brother and her children as co-heirs of all his belongings and as his successors in the rule. In his will he further appointed the larger part to the widow and her children, since the rule belonged of right to his eldest son.

§ 58. Indeed, while the elder son was yet alive, the father had given him entire authority and had designated Dorieus as simply the lord of his possessions in Mitylene. But Dorieus, despising justice and the will of his father, and even his own security—for he would have been safe had he respected the rights of his brother's children and of their mother—unjustly drove off the woman and her children, and seized all their private means and the entire authority, ceding nothing of all this to the children or their mother.

16 Dorino II Gattilusio.

§ 59. She, for her part, took this action very badly, and could not bear the tyranny. At first she tried by arguments to turn him from his greediness, partly in person and partly through able and wise men of the region, and especially through relatives of theirs to whom any dispute over the rule could not but be a great danger.

§ 60. In a kindly spirit they went and counseled him not to change in any way his father's will, nor to wish to domineer over the wife and children of his brother, but to fear the divine Nemesis which travels everywhere and judges the acts of men, sees who are unjustly treated and who are oppressors and what is the inclination of those who have power in such matters. And they advised him to realize that some things are terribly irrevocable and unchangeable.

§ 61. For, said they, it is impossible for those who are wronged to remain silent. They will certainly look after their own rights in every possible way, and will complain of you to the Sultan and traduce you to him, rightly or wrongly. You see where the thing will end. If you are at all solicitous for yourself, or for us, or for the whole realm, be persuaded by those who give you the advice which is best for us all. Share the inheritance and the realm with the children and the widow of your brother, giving them what is just. Thus you will decide on and carry out what is beneficial and best, not only for yourself but for all of us. While for the future you will secure peace and safety to the realm which has fallen to your lot.

§ 62. Although they said all this and much more of this sort to him very often, yet they could not persuade him. The widow, abandoning once for all the hope of persuading him, fled to the supreme authority. She also had sent her maternal uncle as ambassador and spokesman.

§ 63. This man on his arrival, in his sorrow and righteous indignation, and with the desire to punish the perpetrator of the injustice even at the risk of all of them losing their authority—which indeed was what happened—brought before the Sultan many accusations against Dorieus, saying that he was hostile to the Sultan and sought to plot against him, that he was in communication with the Italians, was collecting arms, hiring mercenaries, and planning to place garrisons in Enos and the islands. In sum, said, he, he is aiming at nothing less than a revolt, and if he is not stopped immediately, he may even put into action what he is plotting.

§ 64. With these words and many more like them, he put the Sultan into such a rage and passion that he could no longer restrain himself. The Sultan decided he should wait no longer, that he should not fail to notice what was going on at Enos or altogether neglect a town that had such a reputation in many ways for its great productivity, its favorable situation, its rich soil, and many other things.

§ 65. Enos was of old the largest city of the Aeolians. It was very proud of its glory and wealth and power, and it held sway over all the coasts of the region and also over many islands. It is situated in the best part of the coasts of Thrace and Macedonia, having to the south the Aegean sea and the nearby islands of Imbros and Lemnos and others, and it profits abundantly from commerce with them.

As to the Hebrus River

§ 66. On the north it has the Hebrus River which flows from upper Moesia and has its sources in the Haemon Mountain. It flows through the interior of Thrace and Macedonia southwards, and near Adrianople it becomes large and navigable, receiving the waters of other rivers flowing into it, the Contaezdos, the Agrianes, and the Tearos.

§ 67. Now this Tearos has its sources in the neighboring mountain between Heraeon and Apollonia on the Euxine Sea. The sources flow out of the rock and it is very good for drinking and most beneficial in many ways, as is witnessed both by those who live at its source and also by all who live along its course. The Hebrus flows down and comes near Doriscus, and running past it then empties into the Aegean Sea before one reaches the harbor of Enos.

§ 68. It furnishes many fish of every sort, large and small and fat. And it enables the merchant vessels in that city to carry on by its means commerce with the inland and with some of the cities in its neighborhood.

§ 69. In front of the city there are also some lakes, and still others are near by. These almost make the location a peninsula. In particular there is another lake, a large one, that empties into these. It is situated behind the hill in front of the city toward the north, called Stentoris in ancient times. These lakes contain many kinds of fish and also flocks of geese and of other edible fowl which feed in the lakes and rivers. This city has always had and now has abundance of all these, and all of them good.

§ 70. But the greatest resource and the one in which it overwhelmingly excels nearly all its neighbors both in wealth and in revenue is the salt that is produced there, more and better than anywhere else. By distributing and selling it through all Thrace and Macedonia, the city amasses an immense quantity of gold and silver, as it were in a steady stream.

As to the city of Enos, and what it originally was

§ 71. Thus, then, this city in old times was flourishing and had unbounded wealth and very great power, and was renowned in glory and had many other good things. But in course of time, like the other Greek cities, it fell and was ruined, and remained uninhabited for a long time.

§ 72. But a long while afterward, owing to the productiveness of the region, a part of it was rebuilt by the Roman kings, so that the part near the harbor, where the acropolis formerly was, was again inhabited. In a short time it flourished and became again one of the most renowned and wealthy of cities, with the finest inhabitants and endowed with all sorts of good things.

§ 73. It had as its ruler, about 150 years ago, an Italian nobleman of good family and very powerful, named Gateliouzes. The emperor of the Romans had given him his sister to wife and, as a dowry, Enos and Mitylene.

§ 74. This man brought the city into better condition as time went on, and improved it in every way. And the succession stayed in his family to this fourth generation, till Palamedes and his son Dorieus, from whom now at last the Sultan took away this city.

§ 75. These men and the rulers before them were all accustomed to pay to the ancestors of the Sultan from the time when they first crossed into Europe and took possession of all Thrace and Macedonia, and also to the present Sultan a yearly tax including two tenth parts of the produce of salt plus the other annual taxes. They themselves then enjoyed the rest, according to the permission of the Sultans, and they governed the city. It was possible for the Sultans to have taken it whenever they wished, as indeed they have now taken it.

Expedition of Yunus from Gallipoli against Enos

§ 76. At the Sultan's command, Yunus fitted out ten triremes and set sail from Gallipoli, reaching Eleus the first day. Rounding the peninsula he passed by night through the Gulf of Melas [Saros] and anchored at the cape called Pacheia Beach, a short distance from Enos. It is related that here Xerxes, while conducting his expedition against the Greeks, beached his leaky ships and repaired them, and that he reviewed all his forces at Doriscus. On the very next day, Yunus sailed into the harbor of Enos.

Expedition of the Sultan against Enos by land

§ 77. Sultan Mehmed, with all the royal guard and two squadrons of cavalry, went overland in a fierce storm—for this took place in the very depth of winter. So much were they troubled on their way by fogs and the precipices, and the bitter north winds that many of the footsoldiers were buried in the snow and died, even when they had scarcely left Adrianople behind. On the rest of the road many had their extremities frozen, and lost noses or ears or other members of the body which had to be amputated.

§ 78. Still, in spite of so severe a winter with its cold and snowstorms, the Sultan set out from the city and on the fourth day reached Kypsella [Ipsala], now a large village, but one of the famous cities of older days, about a hundred stadia distant from Enos Bay.

§ 79. The people of Enos, when they saw the fleet come in from the sea into the harbor and heard of the sudden descent of the Sultan on Kypsella, were astounded at what had happened and could not understand the reason for it. They were in the depths of despair and in terrible uncertainty and fear, not knowing what to do. They supposed that they and their women and children would be carried off immediately, for the Sultan was attacking them by land and sea.

§ 80. Now Doreius, their chief, was not there at the time, as he happened to have gone a short while before to Samothrace Island to spend the winter. However, as the most feasible step, they chose the most prominent men among them, and sent them to the Sultan, surrendering themselves and their city to him with the stipulation that they should not suffer harm.

The Surrender of the City of Enos to the Sultan

§ 81. The Sultan received these men who came mildly, and spoke peaceably with them. He granted some of the things they asked for, and sent them back. He also sent with them Mahmud Pasha to take over the city. The next day he himself arrived, and entering the palace of Dorieus, took away all the riches that he found there, gold and silver and other things. And he plundered the houses of the powerful men who had left with Dorieus.

§ 82. After staying three days in the city, having arranged its affairs as he desired, he chose out 150 boys of the highest families. Then he made Murad governor over it, a wise man and kindly in his ways, and returned to Adrianople.

How Yunus entrusted to Kritovoulos the government of Imbros, after expelling the officials of Dorieus

§ 83. Yunus sent a fifty-oared ship to Samothrace to fetch Dorieus, and himself set sail to Imbros in order to arrange affairs there and to expel the officials of Dorieus. But as he encountered a storm, he could not enter the harbor and so proceeded to Kephalos, a cape on the south of Imbros, which was less exposed to the waves and calmer. He then sent a messenger, summoned Kritovoulos, and gave over to him the entire island and its fortresses to rule and to guard.

§ 84. He himself seized the officials of Dorieus, and then set sail for his home in Gallipoli.

§ 85. But Dorieus did not embark from Samothrace in the fifty-oared ship, nor go to Yunus. The reason, as I believe, was that he feared him. Embarking in his own coasting-vessel, he instead sailed to Enos from which he went on to Adrianople. When he came into the royal presence, he was received affably by the Sultan, and was the object of philanthropy and kindness. And he was again given the islands of Imbros, Lemnos, and Samothrace as his own domain.

§ 86. Yunus, however, was angry at Dorieus for not coming to him, which had showed that he feared Yunus would bring him before the Sultan. Therefore, as he thought this act showed arrogance against him, Yunus wished to take vengeance on Dorieus. He secretly sent word to the Sultan while Dorieus was still at Adrianople, saying that he ought not to hand over the islands to Dorieus, since the islanders would not accept him because the man was of malevolent disposition. He added that there was great likelihood of a revolt in the islands, but that Dorieus might be given a place at some interior point for his livelihood.

Remarks as to Dorieus

§ 87. The Sultan was persuaded by these arguments and took back the islands, granting to Dorieus some villages in the Zichna region for a living. Dorieus went there and spent a short time there, but a little later he fled to Mitylene, crossed over from there to Naxos, married in the island of Tenos a daughter of a noble family, and stayed at her home.

Preparation of the Sultan against Belgrade; his expedition

§ 88. The Sultan remained through the winter at Adrianople, collecting a large army and constructing cannon in addition to those he already had. The new ones were more powerful. He also gathered arms and all sorts of other war materials. But he did not disclose his plan, nor did anyone know where he was to make his attack. After careful preparations according to the plan he had in mind, at the very opening of spring he set out from Adrianople and marched through the midst of Thrace and Macedonia to Upper Moesia and to the pass of the Haemon Mountains which is now known as the Sophia Pass.

The Defenses of Belgrade

§ 89. Crossing through it, he invaded the land of the Triballi and, marching rapidly through it and ravaging most of it, reached the city of the Paeonians that lies on the banks of the Ister. This city is called Belgrade. It is very well fortified on all sides and very safe, almost impregnable, partly because of the way it was built, but especially because it is shut off on two sides by the two rivers, the Ister on the north, and the Save on the south which here flows into the former. The city is protected by its lofty and steep banks, and by its very rapid currents.

§ 90. On the landward side, where it was much more vulnerable and could be captured with the aid of cannon, it was defended by a very lofty double wall and a deep and marshy moat, full of water. It also contained a fairly large garrison of Paeonian warriors, all well armed. It was thus impregnable.

Siege of Belgrade

§ 91. The Sultan pitched his camp there, surrounded the city, placed his cannon against it, and besieged it.

Flight of Lazarus to Dacia

§ 92. Lazarus, chief of the Triballi, who had known from the beginning about this attack of the Sultan against his own, immediately crossed the Ister with his wife and children and all his goods, and fled into Dacia. There he remained, waiting for the war to cease.

Look!

§ 93. The Sultan in his siege of the city partly shattered and partly destroyed the wall with his cannon. Then he divided his army into sections and filled up the moat so that it would be easier for the heavy infantry to get to the wall. This work was quickly done because there were so many hands.

§ 94. Those inside the city fought bravely, bringing up stockades and all sorts of defense materials, stones, wood, and other things to the wrecked part of the wall, digging a deep ditch on the inner side, heaping up the earth high, and using every other device for defense. But they never had a chance to complete the work, for the stones shot by the cannon scattered and demolished the materials they had gathered, and broke down the wall.

§ 95. John [Hunyadi], the commander of the Paeonians and Dacians, was encamped beyond the Ister, opposite the city, with four thousand heavy infantry, watching events. When he saw that the wall had been broken down and the moat already completely filled and that the grand battle and the assault by the Sultan and his whole army were very shortly to be expected, he feared lest the city should be captured by force of arms in the attack. Therefore he secretly crossed the river with his soldiers and entered the city and halted, without anybody outside knowing of his crossing.

§ 96. Since all was going in his favor—for the wall had been broken down to the ground, and the moat filled up, and everything else now awaited the assault on the inner wall—the Sultan thought he should no longer delay or put it off at all, but should swiftly attack the city with all the power of his army.

§ 97. Hence, after carefully arranging all his forces, he harangued and exhorted them much in advance, encouraging them to fight, giving orders as to what should be done, and urging them to show themselves heroes. He then led the assault on the inner wall.

The Sultan's attack on the city,
heavy fighting

§ 98. The soldiers with a loud and fearful battle-cry rushed shouting against the demolished part of the wall, ahead of the Sultan. Climbing over this they fought valiantly, trying to get inside.

§ 99. But the Paeonians met them bravely, withstanding the assault and fighting valiantly. There was a fierce struggle there and many were killed in a hand-to-hand fight just in front of the Sultan, his men trying to get inside the walls and capture the city, while the Paeonians tried to repulse them and guard it.

§ 100. At last the Sultan's men prevailed, forced back the Paeonians, and gallantly scaled the wall. In desperate fighting they beat them back, drove them into the city, and poured in themselves. They drove them back in disorder and confusion, and killed mercilessly.

Attack of John against the Sultan's forces

§ 101. Just then John suddenly appeared there, rushing up with his men. With a great shout he quickly frightened and greatly perplexed the Ottomans, repelling the advance. There was a sharp fight, with anger and wrath and great slaughter, both of the heavy infantry and of the Paeonians. Both sides fought well, and excelled each other in determination, acting heroically, the attackers believing they nearly had the city and that its loss would be a disgrace, while the Paeonians were ashamed to be beaten or to lose such a city out of their hands.

§ 102. But the Sultan's troops at this point suffered heavily. They were hit in front and from above from the battlements, and from the houses on the wall they were attacked on the flank. Indeed, on every side the Paeonians attacked them. So, unable to hold out any longer, they gave way, and the Paeonians fell on them immediately with fresh courage and more vigorously drove them back foot by foot, taking some of them prisoner.

Repulse of the Sultan's men, flight, and pursuit by the Paeonians as far as the camp

§ 103. Driving them back from the wall, they followed them clear to the camp and killed some. And when they reached the cannon, they threw some of these into the river and others into the moat, while most of the men turned to looting the camp.

Later attack of the Sultan on the Paeonians; severe battle, their flight and pursuit, and their being again besieged in the city

§ 104. They would have wrought great havoc and looted most of the camp had not the Sultan attacked them in the center with his guard and stopped their onslaught. Fighting desperately, he drove them back brilliantly and pursued them to the walls, pitilessly killing and slaughtering them. Then with vigorous blows he drove them inside, and again besieged them in the city.

§ 105. After that, he left off pursuing them and went back to the camp. Not much had been removed from the camp, since, as I have said, the Sultan fell upon them so suddenly and put them to flight and chased them.

§ 106. A large number of other soldiers had been killed as well as several from the Sultan's guard, brave men. The Governor of Europe, Karaja, also fell, struck by a stone cannon-ball. He was a fine man, one of the most powerful of the Sultan's entourage, renowned for his courage and military skill and valor. It is also said that the Sultan himself was hit in the thigh by a javelin as he fought, but the wound was not severe, merely superficial.

§ 107. The Sultan gave up all hope of storming the citadel. It had already been very strongly garrisoned, and now many more had got in. Therefore he withdrew his army from there. After overrunning a part of Triballia [Serbia], he plundered it and captured forts and devastated villages, carrying off great quantities of booty for himself and giving much to the army. Then, having reinstated Ali there as governor, he returned to Adrianople, for the harvest season was now over.

§ 108. After spending all the autumn there, in the beginning of winter he came to Byzantium. So the 6964th year [A.D. 1456] from the beginning drew to its close, being the sixth year of the reign of the Sultan.

The plot against Lazarus by Michael; imprisonment of Lazarus

§ 109. Lazarus, chief of the Triballi, when he learned of the Sultan's departure, crossed the Ister again, came back into his territory, and remained in Semendria. But Michael, brother of John's wife, who had been left by him as sub-governor of Belgrade, was very furious against Lazarus and in many ways laid ambush against him, wanting to capture him unawares, though no complaint was lodged against him. He did trap him shortly afterwards in one of his fortresses, treacherously arrested him, and put him in prison in Belgrade under a strong guard.

Release of Lazarus for 30,000 gold

§ 110. Lazarus, finding no other way of escape from there, gave Michael gold, begging him to release him. At first Michael refused, and demanded that territory and fortresses be given him—or perhaps he wanted a larger payment. After considerable time had elapsed, and after much entreaty, he gave in and released Lazarus on receipt of 30,000 pieces of gold.

§ 111. So Lazarus got safely away to his own domains. But before he could do more than catch his breath a little, being utterly worn out by his grief, and attacked by a severe disease, he died, leaving as heirs of his domain his wife and Lazarus[17] his son.

§ 112. The latter showed a bad spirit toward his parents. He had grieved his father in many other ways as long as he was alive, but especially when his father was being held as a prisoner in the fortress by Michael, for he was unwilling to get him released by paying the ransom and had done so only

[17] Lazar III.

116

grudgingly and under force, and after being urgently besought by his mother. Now, after the death of his father, he refused to his mother herself any share in the government, but injured her in many ways and was a daily burden to her, demanding his inheritance from his father and the riches which she had accumulated and had concealed.

Flight of Lazarus's Mother, his sister Amirisi, and his brother Gregory

§ 113. The mother, unable to endure his daily insults and various attacks, fled secretly with her daughter Amirisi and her maimed son Gregory, taking along also much wealth. On learning this, her son Lazarus pursued hotly, and caught them in one of the fortresses he owned, for they had not succeeded in escaping into the Sultan's territories, where the Sultan had urged her to come.

Death of Lazarus's Mother

§ 114. Gregory and his sister, however, by hiding or else by getting far ahead of him (for both stories are told), did escape, and fled to one of the Sultan's fortresses. Later they reached the presence of the Sultan, who graciously received them and gave them suitable honors and care.

§ 115. But the mother was captured, through her being old and weak. In a short time, worn out by grief, she died after a brief illness and was buried there.

§ 116. Lazarus her son performed the canonical rites over her. Then, taking all the things she had been carrying with her, he went back to Semendria and had undisputed rule over the Triballi, or whatever remained of them, without any relatives to share it. For his brothers were crippled, and Gregory, as we said, had run away secretly with his sister, while Stephen stayed there but was quiet.

§ 117. So Lazarus, who was young and inexperienced in governing and had no very trustworthy or wise men in his employ—or, if he had, did not show any eagerness to follow their advice—did not rule the country well. Therefore, the affairs of the Triballi suffered and were in disorder and great confusion. In addition to many other mistakes, and by no means least important of all, he did not pay the customary taxes to the Sultan. For this reason the Sultan was very angry with him, and prepared to invade the country as soon as spring came. However this Lazarus lived only a short time after coming to power, and then became ill and died, leaving as his heirs in the government his wife and a female child in her minority.

Death of Lazarus, and despatch of an army by the Sultan to invade all his territory and subdue it

§ 118. When the Sultan leained of the death of Lazarus, he immediately sent an army to Ali, governor of the region, ordering him quickly to invade the country of Lazarus and overrun it all and subdue it. Therefore Ali, when he received this army, levied another, no less in size, from his own province, and overran all that was left of the country of the Triballi. He subdued it and took under his own command the cities and fortresses and all the rest of the country.

§ 119. Advancing to Semendria, he first made proposals for an agreement to the queen and the chiefs, on the basis of the surrender of that city to the Sultan and their enjoyment of the rest of the region by permission of the Sultan, with pledges to be given them. These conditions they refused to accept, but closed the gates and remained inside. So Ali surrounded them with his army, walled them in and shut them up tight, not allowing anyone inside to get out, or anyone outside to go in.

§ 120. The Sultan remained in Constantinople, brought new inhabitants into it, and took every means of caring for those in the City. He erected baths of appropriate beauty, usefulness, and size. He built also splendid residences, inns, and markets all over the City, and caravansaries, and he planted public gardens. He brought in plenty of water, and did all he knew how, to give the City ornamentation and beauty as well as what was necessary for practical life. And he furnished everything needed for the diversion of the inhabitants.

§ 121. Not only this, but he also peopled the suburbs and the country around, transporting many of the Triballi and Paeonians and Moesians from their homes, bringing some of them by force and settling them in this way. He did this because he believed it wise to people all the outlying region near the City, both because of the fertility of the soil—which is good for sowing and planting, and fertile for all sorts of vegetables and fruits—and more particularly because he wanted to provide for the needs of the City and to settle the country which had become to a great extent uninhabited and without houses, and dangerous to travelers. Thus he was busy with this undertaking.

Despatch of a fleet of thirty vessels by the Pope against the Sultan's islands in the Aegean

§ 122. At this time Nicholas, the High Priest of Rome,[18] mustered an army in Italy and fitted out a fleet to cross the sea against the Aegean islands of the Sultan, Imbros and Lemnos and the rest. He fitted out thirty triremes and two large galleons, armed them well, and embarked trained troops in them with arms of all sorts, including cannon. He chose as high admiral his nephew Louis, whom he also appointed as Patriarch of the eastern regions. And he sent them off in the early spring.

Surrender first of Lemnos to the Italians

§ 123. Sailing from Italy he arrived at Rhodes and, after a brief stay there, set sail and went to the islands of the Sultan. He reached Lemnos first, made a landing, and took possession of it by agreement, for the people of Lemnos surrendered immediately, as did also the Sultan's garrison which he had placed on the island. It was a guard of one hundred trained warriors from the Janissaries of his personal bodyguard, with their commander, Murad by name, who was in command of the entire island.

18 The Pope in 1457 was actually Callixtus III. Possibly preparations had been begun by Nicholas.

Capture of Thasos by the Italians

§ 124. After a stay of eight days in Lemnos, during which he made suitable arrangements there and left a sufficient garrison under Loizos as its commander, Louis sailed away and went to Thasos. Here he landed, and began negotiating first for a voluntary surrender of the island and of the garrison in the fortress at the harbor. But as he could not persuade them to this, he surrounded the fortress with his army and attacked furiously on all sides. And bringing up ladders against the wall, and cannon, he captured it by force, at the first assault. Some of the guards he killed; others he captured alive. There were in the fortress sixty of the Sultan's soldiers.

§ 125. He so frightened the people in the other towns by this that he received these by surrender, for they gave up themselves and their fortresses without a battle. So, having gained control of the whole island and thoroughly subdued it in fifteen days, he put matters in good order there, left a garrison, and sailed away for Lemnos with all his fleet, taking with him the men he had captured alive in the fortifications.

Arrival of Kontos in Imbros with ten triremes and his departure having accomplished nothing

§ 126. When he reached Lemnos, he sent ten triremes to Imbros, with a certain Kontos as commander. Louis himself stayed only four days in Lemnos. On the following day he took the Sultan's soldiers whom he had captured in Lemnos and Thasos, as many as had not died, and sailed away with the rest of the fleet to Rhodes.

§ 127. Kontos reached Imbros with his ten triremes and made proposals to Kritovoulos, the lieutenant of this island, as to the surrender of the island, handing him also letters from Louis on this subject.

§ 128. Kritovoulos received him in a friendly manner, gave him many presents, greeted him with mild and affable words, used every other possible means of mollifying him, and sent him away in peace satisfied with the words he had heard and making no further demands. Neither did Kontos meddle at all in affairs, or carry out the purpose of his coming.

§ 129. Kritovoulos entrusted to him letters to Louis regarding the situation. They were written in a friendly spirit. So the man sailed away to Rhodes.

§ 130. Just at this time the autumn ended, and the 6965th year [A.D. 1457] from the beginning came to its close, which was the seventh year of the reign of the Sultan.

PART III

S U M M A R Y

Containing the war with the Peloponnesians, and the first and second invasions by the Sultan, and the complete overthrow and enslavement of these peoples, and other events of the period. Covering three years [A.D. 1458-1460].

Reasons for the Expedition of the Sultan into the Peloponnesus

§ 1. During that same winter, the Sultan sent ambassadors to the Peloponnesus, demanding from the local authorities there the yearly taxes, which in fact they owed for about three years. For the Despots of the Peloponnesus,[19] after Byzantium had been captured, had been confronted with a plot and revolt of the Illyrians [Albanians resident] in the Peloponnesus against them, and called on the Sultan to come to their aid, promising to pay him an annual tribute from the Peloponnesus of six thousand gold staters.

§ 2. The Sultan had agreed to a military alliance with them, and had furnished them with a considerable army, with the aid of which they fought the Illyrians and completely subjugated them, compelling them to pay tribute. However, after that they did not readily pay their taxes on the demand of the Sultan, getting up empty excuses all the time and making inexcusable delays. They did this even though they themselves received from the Illyrians enough tribute to pay all to the Sultan every year. Instead, they wasted it on unwise expenditures for themselves, and cheated the Sultan. Thus he had sent for the money many times but could get nothing from them.

§ 3. Not only this, but the Despots quarreled among themselves and would not listen to the Sultan, but fought and struggled among themselves, and the state of the Peloponnesus was worse in consequence. Of this we shall presently have more to say. Accordingly the Sultan sent his ambassadors to them, demanding the tribute, and at the same time he had these ambassadors investigate the circumstances there.

§ 4. The Sultan was afraid that this internal discord and fighting might bring the Italians, or some other western nation into the Peloponnesus, and he wanted to get hold of the region first, since it was a country very strong by nature,

19 Demetrios and Thomas Palaeologus, brothers of Constantine XIII.

vith remarkably well fortified cities and many impregnable
and notable fortresses abundantly supplied with all provision
for war or for peace. These were favorably located with respect
to land and sea, and the country could well be used to launch
an expedition of Thracians and Macedonians against Italy,
or of Italians against Thrace and Macedonia.

§ 5. The ambassadors, on reaching the Peloponnesus and
delivering the Sultan's message, did not receive the tax.
Furthermore, they found everything there in bad confusion
and far from healthy. Hence they returned and reported to
the Sultan. He considered the conquest of the Peloponnesus
of the first importance, because of the war against the Italians
which he was planning for the near future. This was because
the Peloponnesus was well situated on the voyage to Italy
and had safe harbors that could be bases for large armies and
navies during the war. Therefore he thought he ought not
to wait longer, but set out against the Peloponnesus.

Surrender of Semendria to the Sultan

§ 6. At this time those who had remained in Semendria
:o the last, and in particular the wife of Lazarus, realizing
hat after so long a siege they could not hold out any further,
oluntarily surrendered on condition of leaving the city, safely
nd unhurt, with all their belongings. The Sultan also donated
ɔ Lazarus's wife two towns as her domain in place of
iemendria, one in Dalmatia and one in Bostria [Bosnia].

§ 7. So she took her daughter and all her possessions, and
vent to Bostria. There she married her daughter to the chief
f the Bostrians, giving as her dowry those two towns. After
pending quite a long time there, she later went to Corcyra
Corfu] to her own mother and brothers.

Start of the Sultan for the Peloponnesus

§ 8. After making thorough preparations through the
winter and gathering as numerous an army as possible, both
cavalry and infantry, the Sultan left Adrianople with his
entire army as the spring was just beginning to appear,
and went through lower Macedonia in the direction of

Amphipolis and the Strymon River. He had with him quantities of arms, a variety of cannon, and very much copper and
iron.

§ 9. On reaching the Strymon, he crossed it and skirted
the Keraenitis, or Volvi, Lake. Then, marching on still
farther, he entered Thessaly. Here he encamped and decided
to make a short stay in order to rest his army and to wait
for a second body of troops. He also wished to test the rulers
in the Peloponnesus and determine whether possibly they
would submit when they learned of the Sultan's expedition
against them, and pay the tribute.

§ 10. It was also said that if their ambassadors had then
gone to the Sultan, bringing the tribute and suing for peace,
they would have succeeded, and the Sultan would not have
advanced any farther nor attacked them, for he had other
urgent business.

§ 11. But after waiting there many days, he received no
sign from the Peloponnesus. Consequently, since the army
was rested and the expected reinforcements had arrived, he
left Thessaly, going through its central part. Passing through
it and Phthiotis, he crossed the mountains of the latter and
of Achaia, traversed the intervening rivers, Spercheius and
Peneius,[20] and reached Thermopylae where he went safely
through that pass.

§ 12. Marching down into Phocis and Boeotia and Plataea,
he encamped there, near the Asopus River. Then he sent
scouts to spy out the Kithaeron Mountain passes which lead
to the Isthmus, for he feared that the Peloponnesians might
have started earlier and seized the passes, in which case the
crossing of the Isthmus would have been difficult for him.

How there came ambassadors from the Despot Thomas, but went back without accomplishing anything

§ 13. Here there arrived ambassadors from the Despot
Thomas, bringing as part of the tribute 4,500 gold pieces
and begging for a treaty of peace. But this was altogether
useless by that time, and indeed untimely, and I might add,

[20] The order of the two streams is reversed.

wholly foolish. It resulted only in the loss of the sum which they had brought, and did not succeed in making peace.

§ 14. The Sultan accepted the tribute money from the ambassadors. "But the treaty," said he, "we will make when we are inside of the Peloponnesus." This he said deriding and mocking them for their imprudence and tardiness, for they ought to have taken this step, along with the payment, when the Sultan had called for them and the time was favorable.

§ 15. When the scouts returned and reported that there was no obstacle in the passes, he broke the camp on the Asopus and went to the pass, traversing it without any difficulty and coming out on the plain before the Isthmus and the wall. There he encamped for one day. The next day, with his whole army in battle array, he invaded the Corinthian territory and pitched camp not more than about four stadia from the city, just as the grain was ripening.

Invasion of Corinthia by the Sultan and Siege of Corinth

§ 16. The next day he took with him some of the best and most representative generals and officers and went around the hill and the city itself in order to ascertain which were the wholly impregnable parts of the location and which where more or less liable to attack. It seemed to him that the city was exceedingly strong, as indeed it was. The place is very high and steep, with precipices all around it, and there is only one approach to the city. It itself is steep, and enclosed and fortified by a triple wall. The Acrocorinthus is wholly impregnable, built on the lofty summit of the hill and fortified by very strong walls.

§ 17. Accordingly he thought best to make an offer first to those in the city to come to an agreement and surrender it. So he sent messengers to them. But as he did not receive assurances, he first ravaged and laid waste the surrounding country, that is, the gardens, fields, vineyards, and all the other lovely and fruitful places, and destroyed the growing grain. Then he surrounded the people with his army, shut them securely inside the city, and set up his siege guns.

§ 18. When he had surrounded and besieged the city for many days without making any progress, he realized that the siege would take a long time. The cannon did not hit the wall properly and could do it no harm because they were so far away that the balls lost their force and struck the wall very feebly. This was because the country was so steep and rough that they could not get near enough to the wall to batter it with such force and velocity as to destroy it.

§ 19. Even if they should completely batter down the wall, still access to the citadel and the city would be quite impracticable, for it was surrounded on all sides by steep precipices and crags which inspired terror and great cowardice in any persons wanting to attack from below, inasmuch as they would have missiles hurled at their heads from above from the summits on both sides.

§ 20. Although the Sultan made frequent and violent assaults against it, he was repulsed. So, since he realized that he could not capture the town either by armed assaults or by cannon-fire or in any other way except by starvation and a prolonged siege, he judged it unwise to delay his other matters so long, or rashly to waste time. Instead, leaving there half his army under Mahmŭd to besiege and guard the city in order not to allow those inside to leave or those outside to enter, he himself took the rest of his troops and went off against the remaining places.

March of the Sultan toward the interior of the Peloponnesus

§ 21. First, then, he captured in a few days all the fortresses around Corinth, some by force of arms, others by terrorizing and frightening them, and the rest by persuasion. Then he went on into the interior of the Peloponnesus, devastating and pillaging everything in his path. He leveled down and smoothed off the rough and difficult and rocky parts of the country and of the passes, and captured the most impregnable fortresses, conquering them and razing them completely to the ground.

Surrender of Tegea to the Sultan

§ 22. He arrived at the city of Tegea, which people call Oenavmochlion, and pitched his camp. He built a stockade around the city, surrounded it with his army, and besieged it for a few days. After that, Demetrius Asanes, sub-prefect of the town, came to negotiate with the Sultan as to terms for the surrender of the city. They agreed, and the Sultan took the town on the stipulated terms. Similarly, not a few other fortresses in the neighborhood surrendered to him.

§ 23. The rulers of this interior portion of the Peloponnesus were waiting in battle array at Amyklaeus. When they learned that the Sultan had arrived near Tegea, they broke up immediately and fled and went off, Thomas to Mantinea, where his wife and children were, and Demetrius to Epidaurus on the sea, now called Monembasia. There they waited, anticipating the end of the war.

March of the Sultan against Patras

§ 24. After the Sultan had spent a few days in Tegea, setting things in order, he left a guard of soldiers there and in the other fortresses, and started for Patras in Achaia, by way of a rugged and steep road which was cut up and shut off by many difficult and well-nigh impassable spots.

Flight of the people of Patras before the arrival of the Sultan

§ 25. Nevertheless he advanced quickly and carefully, plundering and destroying everything in his path. The people of Patras, when they learned of the advance of the Sultan against them, were seized with terror and dread. They abandoned the city and their property, and precipitately fled with their wives and children, some to the Venetian cities in the interior of the Peloponnesus, and others crossing over to Naupactus. They left only the citadel guarded.

Surrender of the Acropolis of Patras
to the Sultan

§ 26. On reaching Patras, the Sultan found the city deserted and empty of men. Accordingly he let loose the army to plunder what is contained. He surrounded the acropolis with his troops, placing stockades all around it, and he set up his cannon and besieged it. The guards inside, fearing the danger from the cannon and that the wall should be demolished and they themselves captured by the armed forces and be in danger of their lives, surrendered to the Sultan on condition of having no harm befall them. And in fact they suffered no harm.

§ 27. Thus the Sultan took the citadel and placed a guard there. Then he made proclamation to the people of Patras that whoever wished might return immediately to the city and live there with a certain term of years immunity from taxation and with the return of their possessions. He was exceedingly pleased with the city and region, for it was very fertile and enjoyed an unusually fine location in a good part of the Peloponnesus at the mouth of the Crissaean [Corinthian] Gulf. It was separated from the mainland only by the strait between, and it greatly benefited from this, besides enjoying many other advantages. Hence the Sultan was very anxious to repopulate and safeguard the city, and in this he succeeded.

§ 28. He stayed there several days, and captured all the surrounding fortresses, putting guards in them as well as in the city. Then he sent part of the army to overrun Elis and Messenia and all the surrounding places, and to pillage them mercilessly and bring all the booty to him.

Surrender of Vostitsa to the Sultan

§ 29. He himself with the rest of the army went along the shores of the Crissaean Gulf towards Corinth. There he attacked a well-known town on the seashore, now called Vostitsa. He so terribly frightened the inhabitants by his sudden assault that he took this town also by surrender, and placed a garrison in it.

§ 30. Then he left there and marched on Corinth, carrying before him everything he encountered, like a torrent. He subjugated all, enslaving one place and completely destroying another.

§ 31. When he reached Corinth, the Sultan found it still besieged but not yielding at all. After he had consulted with Mahmud and the other governors and generals, they came to a complete agreement that they should attack the city by force of arms, using all the means they had and trying in every way to capture it, if possible, by assault and by weapons.

§ 32. Already a part of the wall around the approach and the gates had been demolished by the cannon. They did not want to waste any more time in vain or sit around the city any longer, accomplishing nothing. The siege had already lasted long enough, for the army had been there four months and the soldiers were wearied by their hardships for so long a time. The animals, too, were perishing of hunger, since the whole country had been ravaged. There were also many other circumstances that annoyed them greatly, and so they were eager to make some move, one way or another.

Fierce assault of the Sultan on Corinth, and its failure

§ 33. Now when the Sultan had made his preparations and had assigned all the forces their positions and armed them well, he urged on all the commanders—the governors and generals and division commanders, yes, and the soldiers themselves—and incited them to battle, calling on them to show themselves brave men. He made a powerful assault on the city, and there followed a fierce battle near the gates and the entrance, this being the only point that seemed vulnerable, for all the rest of the city was wholly impregnable.

§ 34. There was a fierce attack here, with shouting on both sides and death and wounds, for the fighting was now hand-to-hand. The heavy infantry attacked the defenders vigorously, got inside the gates of the ruined outer wall, and mastered the wall itself.

§ 35. But when they tried to force the second wall also, and get inside it, they suffered terribly. The enemy struck them in front with long spears and javelins and axes, and hurling down stones on their heads from above, from the peaks on either side, especially on the right hand. This pressed them particularly hard, and at last they gave way and were powerfully driven off by those inside, and forcibly thrust outside of the wall. Not a few of the heavy infantry died there. They were especially heavily hit by the men above them who had hurled down immense stones from a height when they were forcing an entrance and advancing with great courage.

§ 36. Seeing this, the Sultan immediately signalled to them to retire and get beyond range of the javelins and withdraw from the fight. He bade them not to struggle in vain or to endanger themselves. For, said he, not arms and human bodies, but famine is the strongest enemy of this city, and that, like a whetstone, will wear it down quickly without any danger to us.

§ 37. The Sultan had decided he would never abandon this city, but would besiege it until he had successfully starved it out. He believed that as soon as he had captured this place, he could gain the whole Peloponnesus without a battle—as indeed resulted. Just at this juncture the soldiers who had been sent off for plunder arrived, bringing very rich booty from Elis and its neighborhood.

§ 38. They are reported to have brought, of animals, about 150,000 sheep, oxen, and horses, and of men, women, and children, more than four thousand. The former, that is the sheep and oxen and horses, he distributed to the whole army. The men, women, and children he sent to Constantinople so as to people all the outskirts of the city.

§ 39. As for the Corinthians, after four months of siege their grain had failed them, and other essential supplies also, and they were hard pressed by famine. Still they resisted, and never thought of making terms, for they feared lest the Sultan, much enraged by the long continuance of the siege, might wreak some dire vengeance on them, particularly so because, though he had often requested them to make terms, they had not been willing to listen and had repulsed him.

Arrival of Asanes at Corinth, and his secret entry into the city

§ 40. At this juncture there arrived Matthew Asanes of Sparta, whom the Despot Demetrius had sent to them as a helper. He was to attempt, if possible, to bring about an understanding between the Sultan and the Despots themselves, and make a treaty with him on as favorable terms as might be, but he was not to surrender Corinth to him.

§ 41. This man had with him seventy soldiers, and they had ten medimni of wheat, which they carried on their shoulders, each man carrying three choenixes.[21] These men knew a path on the most inaccessible side of the mountain and of the town, unknown and impassable to most, very steep and rough and hard to traverse, but leading up to the Acrocorinthus. By concealing themselves at night, they scaled the rock with great difficulty and danger, scrambling up and helping and holding each other. Some of them pulled themselves up with ropes tied around them, and so they entered the citadel.

§ 42. When they saw Asanes and his followers, the Corinthians were not a little encouraged and relieved, thinking that he was come to help them in many ways. They especially hoped that he would make suitable conditions for them with the Sultan.

§ 43. But when Asanes came into the town and saw how terribly the Corinthians were suffering from famine, and how unable they were to resist, he sent a messenger to the Sultan to treat concerning conditions of agreement and the surrender of the city.

Treaty made by Asanes with the Sultan for the Despots

§ 44. The Sultan agreed to these conditions, and gave

---

[21] The *medimnus* is listed at ca. 52½ bushels, and the *choenix* at ca. 2 quarts, but such measures varied widely from place to place.

him assurances. So Asanes went out and made terms and a
treaty with the Sultan. He surrendered to him the city and
the Acrocorinthus, with the provision that the Corinthians
were to remain where they were, safe and unhurt, and were
merely to pay tribute.

§ 45. Further, it was agreed that all the territory of the
Peloponnesus, as much of it as the Sultan had entered with
armed forces, and all the cities and fortresses he had captured,
should be subject to him. This constituted a third part of the
Peloponnesus. The remainder was to belong, all of it, to the
Despots. They were to pay an annual tribute of three thousand pieces of gold, and the Sultan would agree to a firm
peace and friendship with them, and be their ally and helper,
if anyone should make an armed attack on them.

§ 46. When Asanes had made these arrangements and
agreements with the Sultan, he returned to the Despots to tell
them what he had accomplished, and to give them the conditions for peace with the Sultan. They accepted the agreement on these matters willy-nilly, but it seemed very hard
to them to accept, not so much the other conditions, but the
surrender of Corinth which was so irreconcilable to the rest
—a very strongly fortified and important city, situated so
advantageously on the Isthmus, and having a citadel such as
the Acrocorinthus. But what could they do?

Note

§ 47. The Sultan took over Corinth and brought into both
the citadel and the town, a large garrison of chosen men, 400
from his bodyguard of Janissaries. He placed one of his most
faithful men in command of this garrison. He also furnished
it well with food and arms and cannon, and with every other
essential.

§ 48. The other cities that he had taken, both in the interior and on the coast, and the fortresses which he considered
essential to him, he repaired and completely armed with garrisons, commandants, food, weapons, arrows, and everything
necessary. But some of the fortresses which he deemed un-
suitable he demolished entirely.

§ 49. The inhabitants of these, men and women and children, he sent to Constantinople all unharmed, with others from other places, so as to people, as I have said, all the suburbs of the City.

§ 50. When he had put everything in good order in the Peloponnesus, as he had planned it, and had left Omar [Amaras] as governor-general over that whole region, he disbanded the army, after first praising them highly and giving them presents, and honoring the notables among them with gifts and emoluments and positions and many other things.

Arrival of the Sultan at Athens; his inspection of everything in it

§ 51. He himself left Corinth at the beginning of autumn (for the summer had already ended) with his court and with some of the high dignitaries, left the Isthmus and reached Athens by way of Megara. He was greatly enamored of that city and of the wonders in it, for he had heard many fine things about the wisdom and prudence of its ancient inhabitants, and also of their valor and virtues and of the many wonderful deeds they had done in their times when they fought against both Greeks and barbarians. So he was eager to see the city and learn the story of it and of all its buildings, especially the Acropolis itself, and of the places where those heroes had carried on the government and accomplished those things. He desired to learn of every other locality in the region, of its present condition, and also of the facts about the sea near by it, its harbors, its arsenals, and, in short, everything.

§ 52. He saw it, and was amazed, and he praised it, and especially the Acropolis as he went up into it. And from the ruins and the remains, he reconstructed mentally the ancient buildings, being a wise man and a Philhellene[22] and as a great king, and he conjectured how they must have been originally. He noted with pleasure the respect of the inhabitants of the city for their ancestors, and he rewarded them in many ways. They received from him whatever they asked for.

[22] This word stands in the margin of the manuscript and apparently is an after-thought of the author.

§ 53. After spending four days there, he set out thence on the following day and went through Boeotia and Plataea, looking all over the Hellenic sites and examining them carefully and getting information about them all.

Arrival of the Sultan at Euboea; his careful investigation of it, and of the ebb and flow of its tides

§ 54. Proceeding according to plan, he arrived opposite Chalkis, in Euboea. There he saw the frequent currents and changes of the Euripus, the peculiar situation of the island, its condition and its excellence, and the way in which it was closely related to the mainland, with only a very narrow strait between. Rather, the whole island was like a peninsula, separated from the mainland by this very narrow stream, as if by a river, and with a bridge connecting the two.

§ 55. When the Euboeans saw the Sultan approaching them with a large force, they were at first apprehensive lest it might be with the purpose of harming them. But later they prepared presents of great value for the Sultan, and went out and met him. He received them graciously, spoke peaceably with them, and sent them back again.

§ 56. Then the Sultan left there, and always traveling rapidly forward, reached Pherae in Macedonia[23] in ten days. There he stayed a few days. Then, as soon as he and his army had thoroughly rested, he broke camp there and arrived in Adrianople about the middle of the autumn.

§ 57. When he got there, he immediately sent for Ismail, governor of Gallipoli and admiral of the entire fleet. He ordered him to fit out as soon as possible a fleet of 150 ships and to sail to Lesbos and to Mitylene. He was to attack the whole island and pillage and sack and destroy it as thoroughly as possible.

§ 58. The rulers of this island, two sons of Dorieus, who had inherited the whole island and its control at the death of their father, were always quarreling with each other and plotting revolt. And when they had seen the thirty triremes

23 Presumably Beroea (Veria).

of the High Priest of Rome coming from Italy under the command of Louis,[24] admiral and commander-in-chief, they immediately had revolted and made an agreement with him, overthrowing their allegiance to the Sultan to whom they would no longer pay the customary tribute which they had brought each year.

§ 59. Not only this, but even before that they had received pirate ships into their harbors, and by secretly giving them provisions and allegiance, they had been doing injury to that entire part of the Sultan's coastline and pillaging the ships that sailed out on commercial trips. So the Sultan was angered at them because of this, and sent his fleet there.

Expedition of the Sultan's fleet to Lesbos and Mitylene, and destruction and devastation of the inhabitants, with the carrying away of much booty

§ 60. Ismail prepared the 150 ships as quickly as possible, and loaded them with arms, cannon, and heavy infantry in abundance, and horses in cavalry transports. Then, having made preparation of every other sort of military necessities, and put everything on board the ships, he set sail from Gallipoli, and on the third day arrived at Lesbos.

§ 61. He landed at a small coast town, Molybos by name, and first ravaged and pillaged all the environs. Then, surrounding the city with a stockade and with his army, he set up his cannon and besieged it.

§ 62. There happened to be at that time by chance in Lesbos twelve of the triremes which had been sent with Louis. They were under the command of Sergius. Louis had sent them ahead to help Mitylene in case the Sultan's fleet should sail against it, as was being rumored. These ships, however, when they learned that the Sultan's fleet had actually sailed, became frightened and sailed off to Chios to wait there.

§ 63. But Ismail accomplished nothing by his ten days' siege of the city. So he burned the houses which were in front of the city, and then, having overrun a great part of the island of Lesbos and sacked and devastated it and robbed the

24 See above, Part II, sections 122-129.

towns and taken a large quantity of booty, loaded this on the ships and sailed away home to Gallipoli where he dispersed the fleet.

§ 64. Sergius with his twelve ships, once he had learned that the fleet had sailed away from Lesbos, went back again to Mitylene. But because he was roundly blamed and re-proached by the rulers of the city because, though he had come to them as an ally and had promised to help them, he had only put them off with vain hopes and had then abandoned them in their time of need and gone off as a fugitive, he now became annoyed (or rather, he was ashamed), and he sailed off to Lemnos, and later to Rhodes to join Louis.

§ 65. The people of Mitylene, like hurt children, now changed their minds again and sent representatives to the Sultan. They apologized for the things of which they were accused, paid the tribute which they owed, requested a treaty and peace for the future. And they succeeded in managing this, for the Sultan accepted.

§ 66. The inhabitants of Chios and Naxos took the same course later. They feared that they too might suffer as the Mityleneans had suffered, so they sent representatives and paid the tribute they owed, and renewed their treaty with the Sultan.

Arrival of the Sultan at Byzantium and his care of the City and of its population

§ 67. After passing the rest of the autumn at Adrianople, the Sultan came to Byzantium at the beginning of winter. Thus ended the year 6966 in all [A.D. 1458], the eighth year of the Sultan's reign.

§ 68. When he reached Constantinople, he busied himself with his usual cares and gave his entire attention to plans for the City and its inhabitants. First of all, he selected and settled inside of the City as many of the Peloponnesians whom he had brought back as seemed to be better than the rest in their knowledge of trades. The rest of them he placed in the surrounding region in villages, distributing to them grain and yokes of oxen and every other necessary supply they

139

needed for the time being, so that they were able to give themselves to agriculture.

§ 69. After this, he sent to Amastris [Amasra], a city of Paphlagonia and a port on the Euxine Sea, and transported to Constantinople the larger and more able part of its people. He also transported to the City those of the Armenians under his rule who were outstanding in point of property, wealth, technical knowledge and other qualifications, and in addition those who were of the merchant class. These he took from their homes and removed to the City, and not only Armenians, but also such persons from other nations among his subjects.

Command of the Sultan to all able persons, to build splendid and costly buildings inside the City

§ 70. Then he called together all the wealthy and most able persons into his presence, those who enjoyed great wealth and prosperity, and ordered them to build grand houses in the City, wherever each chose to build. He also commanded them to build baths and inns and marketplaces, and very many and very beautiful workshops, to erect places of worship, and to adorn and embellish the City with many other such buildings, sparing no expense, as each man had the means and the ability.

§ 71. The Sultan himself selected the best site in the middle of the City, and commanded them to erect there a mosque which in height, beauty, and size should vie with the largest and finest of the temples already existing there. He bade them select and prepare materials for this, the very best marbles and other costly polished stones as well as an abundance of columns of suitable size and beauty plus iron, copper, and lead in large quantities, and every other needed material.

§ 72. He also gave orders for the erection of a palace on the point of old Byzantium which stretches out into the sea— a palace that should outshine all and be more marvelous than the preceding palaces in looks, size, cost, and gracefulness.

§ 73. Furthermore he ordered them to construct many very fine arsenals to shelter the ships and their furnishings, and to build very strong, large buildings for the storing of arms, cannon, and other such supplies. He also ordered many other similar things to be done to beautify the City and to be useful to the public as well as to be necessary and valuable in his wars and fighting. And in order that all this should be done speedily, he set over the work his most experienced and energetic commanders. Now it was his plan to make the City in every way the best supplied and strongest city, as it used to be long ago, in power and wealth, glory, learning, and trades, and in all the professions and all sorts of good things, as well as in public and private buildings and monuments.

Describing the fine structures of Mahmud

§ 74. In addition to what the Sultan did, Mahmud, the commander-in-chief for Europe, the highest in rank of his courtiers and a very powerful man, being in charge of all the affairs of the government, now erected a very large and beautiful mosque at a prominent place in the City. It was built with dressed stone and gleaming marbles, and with columns of outstanding beauty and size. It was also well ornamented with inscriptions and artistic sculpture and very rich in gold and silver, and it was adorned with many beautiful gifts, votive offerings and other things to be proud of.

§ 75. Around this Mahmud with noble ardor built food-kitchens for the poor, and inns and baths well suited in point of usefulness and beauty and size. Besides, he built grand houses for himself, rich and beautiful, and he planted gardens with trees bearing all sorts of fruit for the delectation and happiness and use of many, and gave them an abundant water supply. He did many such things, precisely according to the wish of the Sultan, and thus beautified the City at his own expense and cost with buildings and monuments useful to the public.

§ 76. At that time the Sultan gave orders that triremes should be built everywhere along his shores, knowing that the domination of the sea was essential to him and his rule, especially for expeditions to far countries. For he knew that in his approaching undertakings naval operations would be of the first importance.

§ 77. He also learned by diligent search and consideration of the history of kings who had had the greatest power, that operations by sea had the greatest chance of success and brought the most fame, and that it was on the sea that those kings had accomplished the greatest things. For this reason he decided to secure control of the sea for himself, because when land and sea are both under one control, they quickly bring that control to its highest pitch.

Prompt submission of Lemnos to the Sultan under Kritovoulos; and the gift of the islands of Imbros and Lemnos by the Sultan to the Despot Demetrius

§ 78. That same winter, Kritovoulos the Imbriote spoke with the influential men of the Lemnians about surrendering the island to the Sultan (for the Italians still held it). Those men accepted the proposal and gave him pledges that they would give over the island when he should arrive. Kritovoulos was one of their closest friends, and they trusted him in such matters. Accordingly they sent secretly, saying they wished to be freed from the burden of the Italians and, most of all, that they feared that if the Sultan's fleet should make an unexpected attack on them, it might do them great injury, for the Italians would be unable to help them. Therefore they wanted to revolt from them and surrender to the Sultan.

§ 79. Kritovoulos took their pledges and went to Adrianople. He also sent letters with all speed to the Despot Demetrius, telling him it was just the time for him to request the Sultan to grant him the islands of Imbros and Lemnos. He stated that the Sultan was ready to turn them over to Demetrius and assured Demetrius that he was strong enough to capture Lemnos and drive out the Italians. For Kritovoulos had already had a letter from the Despot about this.

§ 80. When the Despot learned this, he sent Asanes immediately as a deputy to the Sultan, and asked him for the islands. He received them, promising to pay over to the Sultan for them annually a tax of three thousand gold pieces. Kritovoulos himself was in Adrianople with him at the time, having a share in these matters.

Lo, the boldness!

§ 81. When Kritovoulos had received the letters from the Sultan, he returned as soon as possible to Imbros. And after staying there only one day, he embarked the next day in a despatch-boat and, evading the Italian scouting ships which were anchored or cruising around the island, he sailed across by night to Lemnos.

Entrance of Kritovoulos by night into the city of Kotsinos, and its capture; the expulsion of the Italians

§ 82. He entered the fortress of the Castriotae about the first watch, and they received him. When he had talked with the commander and his colleagues (for the commander was one of those who had conspired with the rest), immediately and without delay he took twenty-five horsemen and reached the town of Kotsinos in the very early dawn. They entered it, for the guards from inside cooperated with them and opened the little south gate. For, as I have said, Kritovoulos had all these men prepared beforehand, and they had been planning this thing with him.

§ 83. When he had entered, the townspeople received him gladly. Quickly and unanimously they gathered with their arms, and imprisoned the Italians, forty-five of them, in the provincial public buildings. These men wanted, to be sure, to resist and to fight, and had indeed made an attack, but they could do nothing. For what could these few do against all the men of the city?

§ 84. At last, as the day broke, these Italians surrendered unconditionally to Kritovoulos, submitting themselves to him to do what he wished. And he let them all go, saying: "If you choose to stay with us, and live on the island, we will welcome you and give you what things you need. But if not, go wherever each one pleases." He sent their chief, Kalavrezos, to Euboea in peace, having honored him with many gifts and honors.

§ 85. After this, Kritovoulos sent a messenger to Michael,

143

Commandant of what is called the Old Castle—this was of old the city of Myrina—and demanded the surrender of the acropolis, promising to give Michael gifts and suitable honors. Now the acropolis of the town of Myrina is very strong and well-nigh impregnable. Since time immemorial it has been renowned for its safety, built as it is high on a crag over the city, protected and fortified by a very ancient high triple wall of huge stones, with the whole city at its feet and dominated by it.

§ 86. For that reason Kritovoulos wanted to entice the man with mild and affable words and the most peaceful means. But the latter, being still young and trusting to the security of the acropolis and also to its strong garrison and its plentiful supplies—for he had with him inside more than enough supplies for a whole year and eighty fully armed men—did not reply in words but drew a sword, in blood, on a sheet of paper and sent that back to Kritovoulos, to show that the acropolis was to be captured only by blood and iron and in no other way. At the same time he added a threat on the paper, and this ironically: "Do not demand the acropolis in that way, for you shall not receive it. But if you are a man, come yourself and take it by force of arms."

Arrival of Kritovoulos at the city of Myrina, and agreement with the commandant for its surrender at a fixed time, acropolis and city

§ 87. Now Kritovoulos spent four days in the city of Kotsinos and arranged its affairs. On the following day he took along four hundred well-armed cavalry and not less than three hundred heavy infantry, and went to Myrina city, pitching camp some distance from the town so that the horses and soldiers should not injure the vineyards and grainfields in front of the city. He then sent a messenger to speak again peaceably to the commandant and try to induce him by mild words and promises.

§ 88. And the latter, seeing the strong force before his very eyes and being none too confident of those inside the city—for he was afraid they might join those outside, or come to an agreement with them and revolt against him from within, so that thus he would lose the citadel and be in personal danger—accepted the terms peacefully and made an arrangement, asking and receiving a delay of three months, so that he might have time to inform his chief, the Grand Master of Rhodes.

§ 89. Now Louis had already set sail for Italy, leaving this man as his representative in the islands. So the commandant secured from him consent to surrender the citadel and town; and for this he gave hostages and pledges.

§ 90. Then, when Kritovoulos had accomplished this, he sent two of the Lemnos commanders to the Peloponnesus to inform the Despot Demetrius of what had happened, and they were to beg him to come and receive, or to have handed over, the island and the towns. Kritovoulos himself waited in Lemnos.

Expedition of the Sultan against the Illyrians living along the Ionian Gulf. Note the strength of their position

§ 91. At the opening of spring the Sultan made an expedition against the Illyrians [Albanians] living along the Ionian Gulf [Adriatic] at the right as one sails into it, near the ancient Epidamnus. These were barbarians who were anciently called Taulantians and Machaones, nomads for the most part, and autonomous and for a long time without kings. They inhabit great and lofty mountains, hard to penetrate, and among these they have many strong fortresses and fortified cities along the shores of the Ionian Gulf. Their entire country is protected on all sides by great abysses and deep forests and steep and precipitous places.

§ 92. A few years before, they had set up over them from their own race a certain Arianos and Alexander[25] as their leaders, and these had held the country strongly in hand, being unwilling to make a treaty with the Sultan or to pay him tribute or to submit to him in any way. Not only so, but

25 Arianites Comnenos and his famous son-in-law, George Castriota, Scanderbeg.

they had often sallied forth from their own country, and by secret attacks and incursions, had injured the Sultan's neighboring domains.

§ 93. Sultan Murad, father of the present Sultan, had previously made an expedition against these people with a numerous and powerful army, and had attacked and beaten them. He had seized some of their passes, overrun and devastated a large part of their country, demolished some of their fortresses, and carried off a great quantity of booty. But he was unable to capture the country or to subdue it entirely. However, he did make a truce with them and impose on them an annual tribute. Then, having captured a very great quantity of booty, which he gave to the army, he had left.

§ 94. For a short time they had faithfully kept the agreements. But soon they rebelled and did not pay the tribute, but made raids into the Sultan's domain and injured it. Therefore the Sultan sent his army against these men. He set out from Adrianople with all his forces, horse and foot, and went through his own territory till in thirty-three days he reached their borders and encamped there.

Encounter of Mahmud with the Illyrians; his victory; his holding of the defiles, and the invasion by the Sultan into the country of the Illyrians, and his pillage of it

§ 95. He immediately ordered Mahmud to choose out three divisions of heavy infantry, and bowmen and supporting troops, the bravest of the fighters in his own bodyguard, and to go by night to the defiles and capture them before the Illyrians should learn that they were coming. But Mahmud, on his arrival, found the passes already held by the enemy, for they had had previous information of the Sultan's expedition. He attacked them, and brilliantly defeated them and took the passes by force.

§ 96. Then the Sultan advanced with his whole army, and invaded their country just as the wheat was maturing. He ruined the wheat crop and also carried off an immense quantity of booty, both men and all sorts of cattle. He captured fortresses, some by force of assault, others by the use of siege operations. Thus he pulled them down entirely, and completely devastated all their country and ruined it all.

§ 97. The Illyrians, who had already occupied the higher parts because they did not dare come down into the plains, when they saw their belongings scattered here and there and ruthlessly destroyed, and since they were also worried about themselves, of necessity had to come to an agreement. Accordingly, sending a messenger, they begged the Sultan to make an agreement with them, they to give hostages and pledges that they would pay an annual tax to the Sultan. This was to consist of a fixed number of children and of flocks of sheep —for they had no money—and also of soldiers to serve in the expeditions of the Sultan. They also promised to be friends and sincere allies.

Treaty of the Sultan with the Illyrians and the taking of hostages; and tribute to be given to the Sultan

§ 98. The Sultan accepted these conditions and made a covenant. Having received the hostages, he took off a very large amount of plunder which he gave over to the army, and went back to Adrianople. It was now the end of summer. There he spent the whole autumn, and as winter drew on, he reached Byzantium to spend the winter there. This was the year 6967 [A.D. 1459] from the beginning, and the ninth of the Sultan's reign.

Arrival of the Sultan in Constantinople, and repair of his palace and of those in the city

§ 99. When the Sultan had reached Constantinople and had rested a bit, he gave attention to the situation in his realm and to arranging and renovating things everywhere, especially what was connected with his own palace and with the soldiers' quarters. He praised all the troops, and he chose out the best of them on the basis of judgment, courage, practice, and military experience. He promoted and plentifully rewarded the brave by gifts of money, offices, and civic rights, as well as by benefactions and gifts, and omitted nobody.

§ 100. After this, he promoted to the greatest and highest of honors and positions in the government the best of the governors, those who had proved most dependable by their acts and who had conducted their districts and provinces as they should, and had administered them well. He replaced them in their former governorships and positions by others and, as I have said, to as many of the extremely useful and important men, as pleased him, he gave fitting rewards.

§ 101. Then he sent out notices and orders everywhere through his domain in Asia and Europe that all who had left Constantinople whether as captives or as emigrants, either before its capture or since, and were living in other cities, should return from exile and settle here.

§ 102. For there were still many such in Adrianople, Philippopolis, Gallipoli, and Bursa and other cities, people who had been scattered through the capture of the city or still earlier and who had settled in those cities, learned men and men of the most useful kinds, men who, profiting by their abilities, had in a short time secured a competency and become wealthy. All these, then, he transferred here, giving to some of them houses, to others building lots in whatever part of the city they preferred, and to still others every sort of facility and needed benefit, most generously for the time being.

Uprooting of the Phoceans and their transfer to Constantinople. Uprooting of the people of the islands of Thasos and Samothrace, and their transfer to the City

§ 103. At that same time he uprooted the people of the two towns of Phocea in Ionia in Asia, and settled them also in the City. And he sent Zaganos, Governor of Gallipoli and admiral of the entire fleet, to the islands with forty ships. When this man arrived there, he removed some people of Thasos and of Samothrace and settled them there likewise. So great a love for the City inspired the Sultan's soul that he wished to see it again established in its former power and glory and brilliancy.

The Sultan overseeing building operations

§ 104. He zealously directed operations on the buildings he was erecting on his own account—that is, the mosque and the palace. He was concerned with the careful collection not simply of materials necessary for the work, but rather of those that were most expensive and most rare. He also took care to summon the very best workmen from everywhere—masons and stonecutters and carpenters and all sorts of others of experience and skill in such matters.

§ 105. For he was constructing great edifices which were to be worth seeing and should in every respect vie with the greatest and best of the past. For this reason he needed to give them the most careful oversight as to workmen and materials of many kinds and of the best quality, and he also was concerned with the very many and great expenses and outlays. Besides, he had many overseers for these things, men who were exceptionally wise and experienced in such matters. Not only so, but he himself also made frequent inspection and watched over the work, doing everything very ambitiously and with excellent taste, altogether in the regal manner. That is how he acted about these things.

Agreement between Kritovoulos and Mikeles and the taking over Palaeo Kastro in Lemnos

§ 106. At this time Mikeles, who held possession of the Cape in Lemnos called Palaeo Kastro, met Kritovoulos and gave over to him the acropolis and the town, receiving from him a thousand gold coins which the people of Lemnos had collected.

Reasons why the Sultan made a second incursion into the Peloponnesus, and seized it all

§ 107. That same winter, the Despots of the Peloponnesus quarreled, to their own damage, and made war with each other for the following reason: the grandees who were under them, men who had domains and large revenues and were over cities and fortresses, were not content with these but, grasping in thought and malicious in act, were always aspiring for more. They sought revolution and were rebellious against each other, made war, and filled all those parts with disorder and uproar.

§ 108. They even drew the Despots into the confusion, by attacking and disturbing each other, for first they would come secretly and accuse the opposite party, as if they were revealing some unspeakable mystery, and so by lies and slanders against each other they tried to stir them up against one another and to arm them.

Note the malice of the men

§ 109. Then later, openly and unashamed, tiey deserted the one side and went over to the other, enticing with them their towns and fortresses. This made the Despots still more furious at each other, and resulted in open enmity although they had indeed attempted once and again, by an exchange of embassies, to solve their differences without recourse to fighting.

§ 110. But as this attempt did not result as they had hoped, because the worse elements prevailed so that they broke up without agreeing, they decided on open warfare; and having once decided, they fought with all their might, invading each other's territory in force and overrunning and pillaging it, burning villages and subduing fortresses, some of which they razed to the ground, and carrying off booty. Thus they despoiled their compatriots in every way.

§ 111. This continued for a long time. After that, the Albanians of that region deserted to the Despot Thomas, and got the better of the followers of the Despot Demetrius by stirring up desertions every day against him, and by surrendering the fortresses. Thus the former prevailed and overmastered the larger part. He exiled his brother, and interned him and his wife and daughter in Epidaurus Limera, which is now called Monembasia.

Despatch of Asanes to the Sultan by the Despot Demetrius

§ 112. Being exceedingly pained at the events, and as there was nothing he could do, since he was in danger of losing all his province, the Despot Demetrius sent Asanes as ambassador to the Sultan, begging him to come to his aid and help him against the baneful influence and tyranny of his brother. This, at least, was how it appeared on the surface; however, there are two versions of this story circulating here. Some say it was not simply for the sake of asking help that the Despot sent Asanes, but that he had promised his daughter to the Sultan and had agreed to give him the whole of the Peloponnesus, asking for himself that he be given another place to rule, in exchange for this, inside the Sultan's dominions.

§ 113. Still others insist that this was not true, but that the Despot was requesting an alliance with the Sultan when he sent Asanes, and asked for men to help him and an army to aid him; and that he was angry with the Despot Thomas and with those of the Peloponnesians who were opposed to the Sultan most of all, and that he had done these things in self-defense, and without the knowledge of the Despot.

§ 114. However this might be, the Sultan heard of the quarrel and difference between them, and of the undeclared war. And in addition since the Despot Thomas had brushed aside the agreements made with the Sultan, and had revolted and made a new alliance with the Italians and called on them for aid, the Sultan was angry at the things that had happened, and feared lest the entire Peloponnesus might pass under the control of others. So he delayed no longer, but as quickly as possible, with the opening up of spring, he launched an expedition against the Peloponnesus.

Expedition of the Sultan against the Peloponnesus

§ 115. So then, starting from Adrianople with all his army, both cavalry and infantry, he advanced swiftly and reached Corinth on the twenty-seventh day and encamped

there, expecting the Despot Demetrius on the third day, for
so they said it had been arranged with him by Asanes.

§ 116. But the Despot had gone from Epidaurus to Sparta,
and did not go in person to the Sultan, but sent Asanes with
very many gifts. He arrived soon, and went in to the Sultan
on the first day, and had quite a long private interview with
him and Mahmud Pasha, and left. But the next day at dawn
the Sultan ordered Asanes arrested, and kept him in prison,
but not in chains.

§ 117. The Sultan then took his army and invaded, not
the hostile country of the Despot Thomas, but the friendly
country of the Despot Demetrius, by proceeding immediately
to Argos. This proved to the majority the accounts already
given, and showed them to be trustworthy, namely, that these
had spontaneously and of their own accord taken the side of
the Sultan, surrendering themselves and the Peloponnesus because of the enmity they had toward the Despot Thomas and
the Peloponnesians. And the rest was a farce and hypocrisy
and a put-up job, as became clear by the events that followed.

Confinement of the Despot Demetrius in Sparta
by Mahmud

§ 118. For the Sultan, as soon as he reached Argos, ordered Mahmud to take a strong force and go by night to
Sparta, and to incarcerate, as it were, the Despot Demetrius.
So he started off, and by traveling all night captured him
at daybreak in Sparta, and confined him there. And he sent
the Sultan's secretary, Thomas, son of Katabolenus, and spoke
in a peaceful and friendly way to him about surrendering
himself and the town, saying it would be for his own good
and that of his followers to entrust himself and the government unhesitatingly to the Sultan, and not oppose him or
hesitate, for that would not be good for him.

§ 119. The Despot replied that first Asanes must be set
free to come to him with the pledges, and that then he would
act according to instructions. All this, as I said, was done in
the open, but they were plotting and doing other things in
secret.

Exit of the Despot from Sparta to Mahmud, and surrender of Sparta, and its acropolis

§ 120. Mahmud gave the pledges to Asanes, set him free, and sent with him the Governor Hamza because he was a special friend of the Despot. So they went into the city, met the Despot, and brought him out to the camp to Mahmud, who received him gladly and in a friendly way and with fitting honors, and took over the city and the acropolis itself.

Reception of the Despot Demetrius by the Sultan, and the great honor and very great gifts bestowed on him by the Sultan

§ 121. The next day the Sultan also arrived, and immediately called for the Despot, and as the man entered his presence, the Sultan honored him by rising from his throne to receive him as he entered the tent, giving him his right hand, seating him by his side, and speaking many peaceable and kindly words. He comforted him in mild and affable terms, dispersing his misgivings and allaying his fears, for he realized that the man was afraid and disturbed. Therefore the Sultan held out to him lively hopes for the future, and gave him reason to take courage, saying that all would be well for him and according to his desire.

§ 122. Then he gave him presents of many kinds—money in plenty, costly robes and garments, also horses, mules, and many other things suited to his present needs. He also sent for his wife and daughter with honors, from Epidaurus, sending one of the royal eunuchs and an officer with a guard of soldiers, with Asanes, to bring them. And in every possible way he greatly honored him and made him comfortable.

§ 123. He spent four days there, repairing both city and citadel and fortifying it, and left there a commander with a garrison of four hundred men of his bodyguard. And he did everything else there that he wished, and put all in order.

Departure of the Sultan from Sparta and his march against other fortresses of that vicinity

§ 124. Leaving there and taking with him the Despot Demetrius, he reached a small town, very inaccessible on all sides, situated on the slopes of the great mountain of Sparta, not far from the city called Kastrion. Encamping here, he first made proclamation to the inhabitants that they should surrender themselves and the town. But they trusted in themselves and in the strength of their fortress, for the place was inaccessible and precipitous and everywhere rough and steep. There was only one path, and that was blocked and guarded by a triple wall. And they numbered about four hundred picked men. So they did not accept the Sultan's advice, but shut the gates and waited.

§ 125. The Sultan immediately gave his orders to the army and made a vigorous assault on the town. But the garrison resisted with great force. The heavy infantry fought bravely, struggling for the entrance and trying to force the ascent. Some of them were counter-attacked by the soldiers above with lances, were hurled down and killed, while others were hit in the head by immense stones from the heights above and crushed and killed, and in the end they were thoroughly repulsed, and not a few of the finest and best fell there.

Second vigorous attack of the Sultan on Kastrion

§ 126. This troubled the Sultan very much. Still, he sounded the retreat and stopped the fight for the time. But the next day at daybreak he drew up the whole army, armed them well, and stirred them up by persuasive and supplicating words, at the same time encouraging them to fight. He promised splendid rewards to those who should fight well, and stated that the fortress would be pillaged. Then he gave the order to attack.

§ 127. The soldiers, with a great and terrible battle-cry and with a shout and a rush, made a mighty attack on the town. There was a great thrust there, and a hard hand-to-hand fight at the wall, with rage and anger and shouting and no little slaughter among the vanguard, each side struggling in disorder, disregarding strict order, killing one another mercilessly, the one party making every effort to get inside the wall while the other stubbornly defended themselves and did not yield.

Capture of Kastrion, slaughter and enslavement and massacre

§ 128. At last the Sultan's troops prevailed. They killed many of them, and forced their way inside the first and second walls, and by fierce fighting drove the men back and swarmed into the citadel. The defenders, driven into a narrow path, and not knowing what to do, since they lacked water and necessary food and were in despair of any help, surrendered to the Sultan unconditionally.

§ 129. The Sultan ordered all the men who had survived the battle, three hundred in number, to be slaughtered immediately, made slaves of the women and children, and destroyed the town.

Attack of the Sultan on the very strong fortress called Gardikion

§ 130. After this he advanced against another fortress called Gardikion, utterly impregnable and very strong for it was a steep and sheer crag near the pass in the Spartan mountain called Zygos. It rose to a great height, and was surrounded on all sides by vast precipices and yawning chasms, fortified and defended, and it had only one path, and that a steep one, leading up to it. Here, then, a great crowd of citizens, men, women, and children, had taken refuge because the place was safe. But this was evidently their destruction.

Siege of Gardikion, and negotiations for surrender

§ 131. For the Sultan marched there and pitched his camp. First he tried to induce them to surrender, as he wanted to let them live and not suffer harm. But as he could not persuade them, he surrounded them with his army and besieged them and guarded them closely, intending to reduce them by siege and hunger and thirst, so as not to lose his soldiers uselessly and needlessly on such precipitous places.

Capture of Gardikion; slaughter and enslavement

§ 132. But they could not hold out more than one single day's siege. Worn out by hunger and thirst, the suffocation of the burning summer heat, and by other privations—since they were such a crowd of men, women, and children herded together on a narrow crag—lacking water and provisions and having neither help from anywhere nor any hope of any, they unwillingly went out to the Sultan and unconditionally surrendered.

Reasons why the Sultan massacred people in such fortresses

§ 133. And the Sultan killed all those men, enslaved the children and women, and razed the fortress. He did this in such fortresses, in some cases from his just anger and wrath; in others, because he had first called on them to surrender, so that there should be no danger to his soldiers in battle, and they had not yielded, but rather preferred battle in which he had lost many brave men.

§ 134. In other cases, where most of the men were Illyrians, because of their bad character and frequent revolts and thievery and brigandage, he wanted to terrify them and cow them, and instill in them the greatest possible fear and dread so that they might never again wish to oppose him, or dare ever to be too impertinent, but be ready to yield to him for the sake of their own safety. And this actually happened.

Advance of the Sultan against the farther parts of the Peloponnesus, and the surrender of the fortresses willingly, and the conquest of the whole region

§ 135. When the Sultan marched on from there and proceeded to the farther parts of the country, he did not have to overcome resistance anywhere, for all yielded readily to him, most of them unconditionally, many of them even anticipating his arrival. Cities and fortresses and the whole of the region, wherever he went, surrendered before his advance and his wrath. Thus all were terrified and gave up, except that a few resisted him through foolish ideas. These were immediately brought to reason by force of arms.

Repair of the suitable fortresses and their garrisoning, and demolition of those unfit

§ 136. The Sultan from that time on gave good treatment to all who complied, and guarded the safety of all and of their possessions, quite unharmed by the evils of campaigns and war. He went through all the Peloponnesus and took possession of it. As many of the fortresses and small towns as he thought suitable and safe and fit for the guarding of the country, he repaired and fitted out with garrisons, commanders, provisions, arms, and everything else. Those which he did not so regard, he demolished. The inhabitants he allowed to remain in their homes and live as organized villages, but some of them he deported, and brought to Constantinople. This was the way the Sultan acted there.

§ 137. The Despot Thomas, when at the beginning he heard of the invasion of the Peloponnesus by the Sultan, repaired very thoroughly some of the fortresses and put garrisons in them, while he himself went off to Mantinea, a small town on the shore, with his wife and children and some of his chiefs. Shutting himself up there, he waited to see the outcome of the war. He hoped that the whole of the Peloponnesus would not give in so easily, for it was a country very strongly fortified by nature, with fortified cities and fortresses well guarded and hard to capture. Hence he hoped that some of these fortresses and towns would hold out and escape capture, and thus he might again have some hope of a refuge in the Peloponnesus.

Flight of the Despot Thomas to Corcyra

§ 138. But when he saw that all of them had been cap-

157

tured, cities and fortresses, some by force and armed attack
and others by voluntary surrender without the slightest force
having been used—when he saw that all of the Peloponnesus
(except for two or three Venetian cities) had been conquered
and held, then he lost all hope of his own affairs, and embarked in two fifty-oared triremes and sailed away to Corcyra
[Corfu] with his wife and children and some of his chiefs.

§ 139. Those of his officers who were rulers of fortresses
or cities abandoned these and fled secretly to the Venetian
cities of Coronea and Methone, and others where they were
safe.

§ 140. Thus the Sultan secured the whole of the Peloponnesus, after carrying out a great and remarkable campaign
in a very short time. For the summer had not entirely passed
when he had captured all points—strong cities and well-
guarded fortresses and little towns, nearly two hundred
fifty in all.

Showing the advantages of this country, and the virtues of its former inhabitants

§ 141. This land is one of the famous and glorious regions
of past history. It has shown many very great accomplishments in its time, and has gained brilliant victories over both
barbarians and Hellenes. It founded many colonies and ruled
over many cities and nations, in both Asia and Europe, and
even in Libya, as well as very large islands. It has shown to
everybody men gifted in intelligence, courage, generalship,
and other virtues, besides being healthy and strong in body,
and very able and perfect in every respect, men such as no
other country has produced except that of the Romans. It
also enjoys a situation strong and well-suited in every way to
the highest degree, whether by land or by sea.

§ 142. Such, then, was the situation in the great and
famous country of Pelops under the Romans; till now it all
had been well governed by them, and had held out great hopes
always, both to Romans and to Italians, even in recent times,
of being useful and helpful. Twice in our own times a wall
had been built across the Isthmus, but it had again been

thrown down and trampled under foot in war by Murad, the father of the Sultan, and so it came to an end.

§ 143. After arranging everything well in the region, according to his own plan, that is, for its guarding and for its general safety, the Sultan left Omer [Amaras] as governor-general of the whole region. And carrying off very great booty for himself, and giving booty to the army also, he left the Isthmus, taking with him the Despot Demetrius together with his wife and his daughter and those of the chief men who had followed him. When he reached Lebadia, he left the Despot behind with the chiefs and with soldiers to wait on and guard him, ordering them to follow slowly and gradually along the road, resting for the sake of the women and children and their baggage and servants.

Arrival of the Sultan at Adrianople. Arrangements for the Despot by the Sultan, and assignment to him of the Islands and of Enos for revenue, and other facts

§ 144. So, leaving there with his personal court (for he had dismissed his entire army), he made his journey and reached Adrianople in the middle of the autumn, and there he stopped. Not many days later, the Despot Demetrius also arrived. The Sultan made it his first business to see to the welfare and arrangements of this man; he immediately sent for Mahmud and Ishak, and in consultation with them granted as a province to the Despot to rule the islands of Imbros and Lemnos in the Aegean and the remaining portions of Thasos and Samothrace together with their revenues. The greater part of the inhabitants of these islands had been transferred to Byzantium. The yearly revenues of these islands amounted in all to 300,000 silver coins minted by the Sultan.

§ 145. Similarly he also gave him Enos, a town of some importance with many advantages, situated on the Thracian coast near the mouth of the Hebrus River, a general trading center for all the neighborhood and surroundings because of its harbors and other advantages, of which we have already spoken. This town he gave him with full power, and with the revenues which Palamedes, son of Gateliouzes, the former ruler, had enjoyed.

Note the generosity of the Sultan

§ 146. These revenues constituted another 300,000 of the same royal silver coin. He also commanded that he should receive yearly, in three installments 100,000 more from the mint at Adrianople. So the total given him annually by the Sultan as revenue amounted to 700,000 pieces of silver.

§ 147. So he gave all this sum to him. And after he had showered many other gifts upon him as well, he left him there. The Sultan himself went to Byzantium at the end of autumn, to spend the winter. So passed the year 6968 by total count [A.D. 1460], which was the tenth of the reign of the Sultan.

PART IV

S U M M A R Y

Including the surrender of the city of Sinope and of all the realm of Ismail, and the surrender of Trebizond and of all its domain and its king; also the revolt of the Getae and their enslavement and the capture of the whole of Lesbos; also the first incursion of the Sultan against the Bostrians, and the destruction and the capture of their whole country. The entire duration: three years [A.D. 1461-1463].

Expedition against the City of Trebizond

§ 1. The Sultan was in Constantinople, and when he had rested a short while, he immediately raised a very large army and fitted out a large fleet for an expedition by land and sea. He prepared arms and guns, and attended to every other military need.

§ 2. This preparation of his and the expeditionary fleet was for Trebizond and Sinope. For Trebizond was in times past the largest and finest city, as well as the oldest of the Greek colonies, being a colony of Ionians and Athenians, situated in a good part of Asia, in a deep bay of the Euxine Sea facing east, along the shore. It benefits by very fine soil, widely extended and fruitful, and it governs a large surrounding region.

§ 3. From its beginnings it has been a common trading center for upper Asia, that is, for Armenia and Assyria and the adjacent country. It prospered in former times, and had great wealth and was very powerful and very glorious. It was among the most famous cities, not only of neighboring regions but also of those far away.

A Change in Circumstances

§ 4. But as time went on, little by little things in Asia altered, and a change took place. Some kingdoms were destroyed or disappeared, while others rose. Some cities and countries were desolated, totally annihilated, while others rose up and were soon populous. So too, this city suffered a like change, for a time, but again recovered very rapidly and returned to her former happy state, unharmed by any of her experiences, and having suffered no misfortune.

§ 5. In later times, shortly before our own, it became the capital of a representative of the royal family of the Romans, the Comneni, who had taken refuge there from Byzantium.[26]

---

[26] The "Empire" of Trebizond endured from 1204 to 1461.

He constructed there many splendid public works, and ruled over many neighboring tribes and cities. And the descendants of this line and their Kingdom had continued till now quiet and without rebellions, their kings always enjoying peace, and the inhabitants tranquil. The countries around either subdued or allied to them.

§ 6. But in these latter years they had internal revolutions and dissensions within the nation, and the city suffered among others. It was near to perishing, and altogether fared badly; for, as I said, the kings and the people rose up against each other, made war, and treated one another badly. Meantime the neighboring nations, taking advantage of the frequent uprisings, revolted against the city and often overran it and pillaged it, doing very great damage.

§ 7. Now, as long as things went well in Constantinople, and the Romans who held it were masters of the Straits, and the Bosporus was closed so that the Euxine Sea was entirely inaccessible to the great fleet of the Sultan, this city and others could resist. Hence, it bore its own misfortunes but guarded its liberty as it might, and was not much injured by its internal strife.

§ 8. But when things changed for the worse, and Constantinople was besieged by the great Sultan and his large and powerful army, and taken, the Strait was in his power. The way to the Euxine Sea and its cities was wholly opened both by land and by sea. Then that city declined as had the others, and became submissive, and the kings in her yielded to the great Sultan and paid tribute.

§ 9. As long as those princes preserved order at home and in their relations with each other, paid the tribute, and did not plot treason, they enjoyed peaceful relations with the Sultan. But when they rose up against one another and gave the tribute only very unwillingly, and further when they allied themselves by marriage with the Kings of neighboring countries of Tigranocerta[27] of the Armenians, and the Medes, and with Hasan the son of Timur [Tamerlane], and of the Iberians [Georgians] as well, and seemed to be plotting

[27] Apparently Koyunlu Hisar, which Kritovoulos mistakenly identifies as the ancient Tigranocerta.

some rebellion, and trying to break their treaties with the Sultan (for they could not hide these acts of theirs), the Sultan was consequently very angry and made this expedition against them, determined to forestall them and gain the mastery over them before they could start a rebellion.

The march of the Sultan against Trebizond and Sinope by land and sea

§ 10. So he made thorough preparation through the winter. When the first signs of spring appeared, he fitted out the fleet for a voyage. He had in fact about three hundred ships of war in fighting shape. They included long triremes, fifty-oared vessels, and armored ships, besides the freight transports and those carrying cannon, and those that went for commerce and for other uses.

§ 11. He placed on board these ships arms of all sorts in very large quantities: small and large shields, helmets, spears, breastplates, darts, and a large number and variety of arrows, both those fired from bows and from crossbows; also many bows and slings and many other things suitable for attacking walls. He also embarked as many men as possible, the strongest and the best equipped, fitted out completely for battle, men of experience. And he put over them admirals for the whole fleet, and as supreme commanders Kasim, the Governor of Gallipoli, and Yakoub, a man of great experience in naval warfare and a very fine admiral.

§ 12. So, after fitting out and arming the entire fleet well, he sent it off; and it sailed up the Bosporus into the Euxine at great speed, with force and velocity, amid mingled shouting and cheering and friendly rivalry of the crews with each other, bringing terror and dismay to all wherever they went, and astounding everyone at the unsual sight.

§ 13. The Sultan also mobilized his European land forces and made them cross over into Asia, cavalry and foot, plus a great quantity of horses, mules, and camels for carrying burdens, and all sorts of material for war, and provisions.

The Sultan crosses from Europe to Asia
with his forces

§ 14. When he had watched the crossing in force, then he himself also crossed over, and marched through Bithynia till he reached Brousa [Bursa]. There he found the Asiatic forces all gathered. So, after spending not many days there, and making some necessary preparations, and fitting out the army completely, he sacrificed a sheep at the tomb of his father, and performed the rightful ceremonies for him in grand style. He adorned the tomb with a quantity of gifts and offerings, and laid a wreath on it. Then he started out from there and went through the region of the Galatians and Paphlagonians.

As to the numbers of the army

§ 15. The army numbered, it was said, sixty thousand cavalry, and not less than eighty thousand infantry, not counting the carriers and other followers of the army.

March of the Sultan against Sinope

§ 16. Having marched his men through Galatia and Paphlagonia and then Cappadocia, he crossed the Halys River and reached Sinope, a coast town, the best and richest of those on the Euxine Sea. It ruled over an immense and splendid countryside and was already a common emporium for the whole region as well as for no small part of lower Asia. It gets the use of many products of the seasons from land and sea.

Remarks about the city of Sinope, and what it was

§ 17. The greatest of these is copper, which is abundantly mined here, and is distributed everywhere in Asia and Europe, and brings in large incomes in gold and silver for the inhabitants.

§ 18. For many years Ismail had been ruler of the city, an able man from one of the noble families of the town;

166

he had inherited the power from his father. The Sultan, then, marched against the city and pitched his camp; he also found his fleet already attacking the harbors,[28] according to plan. For the admirals, arriving first, attacked, and held the harbors and the isthmus, encircling all the city and islet in a circle, by their ships, for it was a peninsula.

Ismail goes out to the Sultan, meets him, and surrenders the city

§ 19. Ismail, seeing the sudden attack of the Sultan, and the land and sea forces surrounding the city and himself, was astonished at this turn of affairs, and considered what he had best do under such conditions. On thinking it over, it seemed to him best to go out and meet the Sultan and learn the reasons why he had made this expedition, and get himself out of the difficulty if he could. So he prepared many very valuable gifts, and went out to the Sultan.

§ 20. The latter received him mildly and cordially, addressed him in a friendly way, shook hands with him, and showed him appropriate honors. Then they talked about the country and the city; and after a long discussion of much that was necessary and right and suitable and proper to the occasion and to themselves, they finally agreed on the following conditions, and parted peacefully, and as friends.

Showing what Ismail received in exchange for Sinope

§ 21. So the Sultan received the city of Sinope and the whole dominion of Ismail connected with it. In exchange he gave him a governorship in Europe called Skopia [Skoplje], on the borders of the Triballi, a very fine and very fertile country in no way inferior to his own in products and territory or in necessities and comforts.

Reasons why the Sultan took over Sinope

§ 22. The Sultan had no complaint to bring against Ismail. But he coveted Sinope eagerly, and got possession of

28 Sinope has two harbors.

;, because it was a city worth mentioning, situated at a favor-
ble point on the Asiatic coast of the Euxine Sea, and with
arbors that were safe and could well serve as bases for his
eet of ships to attack Trebizond and the entire upper shores
f the Sea and the cities there. Besides, as it was situated in
1e midst of the territory of the Sultan, he did not think
: safe from many standpoints for it to be in the power of
ther rulers, and not directly under him.

§ 23. Not only so, but he also feared that Hasan, king of
Tigranocerta and the Medes, might secretly try to get pos-
ession of it, by treaty or by war, since it bordered on his
erritory. And the Sultan knew from many indications that
1e was plotting in every way, and determined to seize it.

§ 24. So for these reasons it was essential for the Sultan
:o capture Sinope. Ismail with all his men left immediately
1nd went off to his new province, and the Sultan took over
Sinope and all the domain of Ismail. When he had arranged
everything there, he ordered Kasim and Yakub to sail with
the whole fleet right to Trebizond, and after seizing the
harbors, to invest the town by land and sea, and keep safe
guard over it.

Expedition of the Sultan up the Taurus;
this mountain, and of what sort it is

§ 25. He himself started from there with his whole army
1nd went through the interior. Reaching the Taurus, he en-
:amped in its foothills. The Taurus is the largest mountain
n Asia,[29] dividing lower Asia from upper. Beginning with
/lt. Mykale and the sea there, and extending from there
nd cutting Asia in two it ends in the Euxine Sea near Sinope.
1nd going on from there again, it unites with the mountains
f the Armenians and the Medes, and through them with
1e Caucasus.

[29] Kritovoulos, like some later classical writers, attempts to use "Tauros"
: a generic term for the mountain systems of Asia Minor. Reference to
map will enable the reader to detect the errors which this involves.

Indicating who have crossed the Taurus under arms, and about Timur, king of the Scythians and Massagetae [Tartars and Mongols]

§ 26. They say that Alexander of Macedon was the first to cross this range with armed forces—although Hercules and Dionysus had, of course, been earlier—when he was marching against Darius, king of the Persians, and against the whole of Asia. After him the next was Pompey the Great with the Romans. And in our days it was crossed by Timur [Tamerlane], king of the Massagetae and Scythians, when he was marching against Beyazid, one of the ancestors of the Sultan. He went armed, indeed, and with an army, but he had for a long time held the passes, and proceeded through country friendly to him.

Showing how Sultan Mehmed crossed the Taurus, opposed by Hasan

§ 27. And now Sultan Mehmed crossed it, but with arms and in war, the third after Alexander, counting the Romans and Pompey. For Hasan, as I have said earlier, being connected by marriage with the Emperor of Trebizond and wishing to be his ally in arms—or, rather, wishing and hoping to conquer Trebizond himself, when he learned of the expedition of the Sultan against the city—gathered a force and went to the passes, intending to prevent the Sultan from crossing.

Of the road by which the Sultan crossed under arms

§ 28. The Sultan learned of this, and allowed him to enjoy himself there with his army, while he himself cut a passage by another route, trackless and rough, and everywhere very difficult and steep, leading straight to Tigranocerta, the capital of Hasan. First he sent out a considerable army of evzones, light-armed men, bowmen and soldiers with small shields, under Mahmud Pasha, and took beforehand the most favorable hills and the narrower and more impassable defiles, and all the difficult places. After that he sent

169

very large numbers of active men to fell the trees and level the rough, steep places and the forests and thickets and bushes of the region through which he wanted to make the crossing, thus securing a wider and smoother passage.

Of the roughness and difficulties of the mountain

§ 29. For this Taurus mountain, although called one mountain, embraces many mountains difficult to cross and difficult to extricate oneself from, and heights stretching above the clouds and steep. There also are very lofty and sheer peaks and deep and yawning precipices, and crags and difficult passes, and chasms, ascents, and declivities, hard and arduous places in plenty. All these make the crossing very difficult and vexatious, and painful and dangerous.

Showing in how many days the Sultan crossed the Taurus

§ 30. But the greatest feat was that a journey of many days, leading through such great and multiple difficulties and through trackless regions which only light-armed and nimble men could achieve—and even these with much difficulty—he made in eighteen days altogether, to say nothing of such an army of cavalry and infantry with heavy weapons and baggage that no one could enumerate; and also horses and donkeys and camels and mules, all loaded. This was a great undertaking, but the Sultan, counting all these as nothing, undertook the crossing.

Note the arrangements of the Sultan, and how he crossed the Taurus

§ 31. So, after setting in order and fully arming the entire army, he made the crossing, having the infantry in the van and wings, always marching on, the baggage in the middle, and the cavalry at the rear, with rearguards and their leaders. He himself was in the midst of the footsoldiers with a few horsemen. And when he passed through narrow defiles, he formed the wings into long thin lines. At times he went forward to the very apex of the point, but when he reached the wider parts of the pass, for a short time he widened out the wings into phalanxes and arranged a hollow square at the front, with the bowmen and heavy infantry as a vanguard, marching in order. The bowmen went with bow in hand and arrows poised on the string, the men being in inverse order, those who shot left-handedly at the right, and those who shot right-handedly at the left. And the heavy infantry marched with their spears on their shoulders, continually pointing them here and there, or brandishing them.

Attempt on Mahmud Pasha, insignificant wound by an arrow from a bow, and capture and death of the plotter

§ 32. So he proceeded each day, encamping by night. He would light many fires in front of the camp and slightly distant from it, and he placed strong guards around, with frequent scouts and outposts whom he placed by daylight in the most suitable places, making the camp secure on all sides.

§ 33. In spite of all this, something inexplicable happened, which not a little disturbed both the Sultan and the officers and the whole army. For a hostile and evil-minded and evil-eyed man, who had no cause for complaint but ought much rather to have been grateful, instigated by his own evil intent and baseness, plotted against Mahmud Pasha. He seized a favorable opportunity for his misdeed and, trusting to the intricacies of the pass and hoping to escape detection, secretly and without anyone knowing it or catching sight of him at all, drew his bow and shot at the Pasha. He wounded him in the forehead, but did not succeed in inflicting a mortal wound.

§ 34. This man was mentally upset by the enormity of his act and his hands were affected by this confusion, otherwise the wound would have been deadly. A very great hue and cry arose at this deed. Both the Sultan and his officers and indeed the whole army were very much upset by this unnatural act, just as if the enemy had made a surprise attack. That very wretched and evil man was speedily seized.

Before he had had a chance for a word of explanation, he suffered the deserved penalty for his daring, being mercilessly cut to pieces by the army. He just escaped having all of them eat his flesh and drink his blood.

The Sorrow of the Sultan for the Pasha

§ 35. The Sultan was moved with boundless sorrow and agony and anxiety for him, lest he should lose so valuable a man, especially at such a time and place of need and danger. He immediately called Yakub, his own physician, a wise man and one with the highest attainments in his art, whether in point of theory or of practice as well as a man who had great influence with him. He asked him about the wound. Learning that it was insignificant, and did not present any danger, he breathed more freely and was relieved of grief. And he gave the physician many gifts, and ordered that the wounded man should be cared for most tenderly. So he, with the necessary care, quickly got well from his wound.

§ 36. The Sultan advanced continuously for seventeen days. Having crossed, with great difficulty and hardships, deep ravines, steep precipices, very rugged regions, and impassable and repelling places, as well as many difficult and vexatious obstacles, and having endured great hardships because of their arms, both he and his entire force got over the Taurus.

Astonishment of Hasan at the Sultan's quick crossing; sending his mother to the Sultan, because he was afraid for himself

§ 37. Descending into the plain, he encamped not far from Tigranocerta. Hasan learned of the swift incursion of the Sultan and how he had crossed so easily by a very difficult road which for the most part was trackless and until that time altogether impassable, how he had crossed with such a large and heavily armed force and with much baggage, and was now marching on his very capital. He was astounded at the unheard-of event. As if struck by a bolt from the blue, he was in terrible perplexity and fear, not knowing what to do. At length, as he absolutely had to do something, he sent off his mother as an envoy to the Sultan. She took very many gifts, apologized for what he seemed to be doing, asked pardon, and at the same time begged to become an ally and friend to the Sultan.

§ 38. The Sultan received her in a friendly way, and rendered her fitting honors and spoke peaceably with her, and made a truce, and agreed to receive Hasan as a friend and ally. Nor would he send her right back, but took her with him, and went on.

Voyage of the fleet to Trebizond; the landing; and the attack by the citizens; their defeat; the siege by land and sea

§ 39. The admirals of the fleet sailed to Trebizond and anchored in the harbors. On landing they joined battle with the inhabitants of Trebizond who had come out in front of the city. Turning them to flight, they made a strong attack and shut them up inside the town. They got control of the whole of the country outside, and of the road leading into the city, and surrounded them with the army on land and the fleet at sea, besieging them and taking strict measures not to allow anyone inside to get out, or anyone outside to enter.

§ 40. Twenty-eight days of siege thus passed. During them there were some sorties by the garrison against the besiegers, in which they proved no less strong than the attackers. However, as they were fewer, and were attacked vigorously by larger numbers, they were soon driven back in, and shut up in the city.

Proposals by the Pasha to those inside the city and to their Emperor, looking to the surrender of the city and of themselves

§ 41. After this, Mahmud Pasha arrived with the land army, one day ahead of the Sultan. He pitched camp not far from the city, and sent as a messenger Thomas, son of

Katabolenus, making proposals to those in the city and to their ruler, looking toward an agreement for the surrender of themselves and the city. He told them it would be better and much more advantageous for them to entrust themselves and their town to the great Sultan with agreements and oaths of good faith. This would be to their good and of advantage to them in general, particularly so to their ruler, his children, and all his entourage.

§ 42. To the ruler he promised that he should have special attention from the Sultan, a large territory, a sufficient income for the sustenance and ease of them all, and everything necessary for his contentment. To the entourage he promised the right to live with their wives and children, quite free from evils, and to enjoy their fatherland and their homes.

§ 43. But he also promised that if, now that the great Sultan called on them to make this agreement, they should not consent, they would no longer be allowed even to remember in future the agreements or treaties, if once they decided in their rage and fury to make war. Instead they would be judged by arms and by iron. Being made prisoners in war, they would suffer death and plunder and enslavement and all the dire consequences of war and capture.

§ 44. The inhabitants and their ruler heard this. They received the message quietly, and said they would agree to the conditions as soon as the Sultan arrived.

Arrival of the Sultan at Trebizond, and parley, and terms, and surrender of the city

§ 45. The next day he himself arrived and encamped before the city. And sending this same Thomas as a herald, he called on them to surrender on the same or similar terms as had been offered by Mahmud. On hearing the herald, they immediately prepared many splendid gifts, and selected their very best men and sent them out with full powers. These went, made obeisance to the Sultan, came to terms, exchanged oaths, and surrendered both the town and themselves to the Sultan. Then they opened the gates and received Mahmud with his army. And Mahmud took over the city.

Entry of the Pasha into Trebizond and his taking over of the city, and the departure of its ruler to make his obeisance before the great Sultan, and his reception and . . . [obliterated]

§ 46. Then the ruler of Trebizond [David Comnenus] with his children and all his suite, went out to do homage to the Sultan. The latter received him mildly and kindly, shook hands, and showed him appropriate honors. He gave both him and his children many kinds of gifts, as well as to all his suite.

Entry of the great Sultan into Trebizond

§ 47. After this the Sultan entered the city. He went about it, noting its situation and the measures taken for its security, the various advantages of the region and the town itself, and also its buildings and the population it contained. He went up to the citadel and to the royal palace, and saw and admired the strength of the citadel and the construction of the palace and its magnificence. He remarked on the high value of the city in every respect.

§ 48. After this he ordered the ruler and all his suite, and also some of the most influential men of the city who had amassed wealth, to go out and embark in the triremes with their wives and children, and all their belongings.

Noting how many children the Sultan took from Trebizond

§ 49. He chose out from the youths of the city and the surrounding region about one thousand five hundred and sent them on board the triremes. Then, having munificently rewarded the commanders of the fleet, namely, the captains of the triremes and the admirals, and even the helmsmen and the overseers of the rowers, and the rest, he ordered them to weigh anchor. So they sailed away.

§ 50. He then selected one of the admirals of the fleet, Kasim, the Governor of Gallipoli, and gave him the governorship of Trebizond. He gave him also from his own bodyguard four hundred chosen men as a garrison. After spending not many days there and arranging everything in the city according to his own ideas, he left for home by the same route.

Dismissal of Hasan's mother by the Sultan with gifts and honors; the embassy of Hasan to the Sultan, and their friendship and alliance with each other

§ 51. When he came to Hasan's country, he sent back Hasan's mother with many gifts and honors. He also sent emissaries with her to her son Hasan, renewing his pledges and saying, as he had said before, that he wanted him as an ally and friend. Hasan in turn sent emissaries to the Sultan with gifts, congratulating him on his successes, expressing thanks for the honors done to his mother, and assuring him of his friendship and alliance.

Arrival of the Sultan in Byzantium

§ 52. The Sultan left there and, marching swiftly on, crossed the Taurus safely. Passing through all the intervening country in a total of twenty-eight days, he arrived in Brousa [Bursa]. There he disbanded his army, and he and his companions rested a few days. After that, as the autumn was ending, he went to Byzantium. And the 6969th year in all, ended, the eleventh of the reign of the Sultan [A.D. 1461].

How he cared for the ruler of Trebizond

§ 53. Such was the manner in which operations were carried out around Sinope and Trebizond, notable cities and well known in our own times. And Sultan Mehmed, when he reached Constantinople, first of all attended to making provision for the ruler of Trebizond. He gave him and his companions a region sufficient for their support, somewhere near the Strymon River. From this he received a yearly income of an estimated 300,000 pieces of silver.

Of the philosopher George Amiroukis and how the Sultan received him and honored him

§ 54. Among the companions of the ruler of Trebizond was a man named George Amiroukis, a great philosopher, learned both in the studies of physics and dogmatics and mathematics and geometry and the analogy of numbers, and also in the philosophy of the Peripatetics and Stoics. He was also full of encyclopedic knowledge, and was an orator and a poet as well.

§ 55. The Sultan learned about this man and sent for him. On getting well acquainted with his training and wisdom, through contact and conversation, he admired him more than anyone else. He gave him a suitable position in his court and honored him with frequent audiences and conversations, questioning him on the teachings of the ancients and on philosophical problems and their discussion and solution. For the Sultan himself was one of the most acute philosophers.

§ 56. After this, he gave himself anew to efforts in behalf of the City, taking special pains to increase its population and also for its general beautifying, including everything ornamental and useful. He erected houses of worship, naval arsenals, theaters, marketplaces and other buildings. In addition, he introduced into it all the different trades and crafts, searching in every direction for men who knew these and were skilled in them, then bringing them in and settling them, sparing no expense or cost for this end. He was determined to make the City self-sufficient in every respect, not dependent on any outside source, whether in point of ambition or need or adornment or splendor.

The revolt of Drakoulis [Drakula], chief of the Getae [Vlachs]

§ 57. In this situation, then, while the Sultan was putting things to rights in the City, in the winter, it was announced that Drakoulis, chief of the Getae[30] was striving to head an insurrection, and that he had gathered a considerable army,

---

[30] Vlad the Impaler, Voyvod of Wallachia.

with horses and weapons, to rebel against the Sultan who had previously granted him that principality.

§ 58. This man and his brother had fled when John the Getan [Hunyadi], ruler of the Paeonians and Dacians, had come in with a considerable force and had killed their father and given the governorship to another man. The father of the present Sultan had then welcomed these two fugitives who fled to him. He very nobly nourished them in the palace while they were yet young boys, and on his death he left them to the Sultan his son. He, too, brought them up with great care and honor, and provided for them royally.

§ 59. Then when a revolution occurred as to the ruler-ship over the Getae, and the man who had been governing the region was badly defeated, the Sultan took this Drakoulis, and at great expense forcibly set him as ruler over all the country of the Getae. He exchanged pledges and oaths with him, specifying that he should guard unsullied and pure his affection and good will toward the Sultan, and also the promises and treaty which they had made.

How Drakoulis crossed the Ister and devastated the country around Nicopolis and Vidin

§ 60. But Drakoulis remained faithful to this treaty only a short time. Then, forgetting it all and being evil-minded toward the one who had trusted him, he revolted against the Sultan. First, he secretly crossed the Ister with a large and powerful army, and invaded all of the adjacent section of the Sultan's domains, namely, around Nicopolis and Vidin. Then, after capturing much booty and killing many people, he crossed the river again and returned to his own country.

§ 61. On this, the Sultan sent messages to him to remind him of his obligations, and to try to find out the causes of the revolt. But Drakoulis, even before finding out the object of their coming, seized them and killed them by impaling them, and uttered many blasphemous threats against the Sultan.

Advance of the Sultan against the Getae, his
crossing of the Ister, and overrunning of all
their country, and devastation of it

§ 62. The Sultan could not bear this insult, but was justly
indignant. He immediately gathered a very large army and,
after thorough preparations during the winter, crossed the
Ister in the early spring. Once he had crossed, he overran in
a few days practically the whole country of the Getae, sack-
ing and plundering it, coming on like a torrent and sweeping
all before him. He captured fortresses, pillaged towns, and
carried off immense booty.

§ 63. That rash and arrogant man did not wait for the
swift advance of the Sultan, but fled immediately. He occupied
the most inaccessible mountainous parts of the country, and
awaited the outcome of events. And the Sultan wreaked his
will on the country. In the end he appointed Rados, the
brother of Drakoulis, as commander and ruler of the Getae.
This Rados he had with him.

§ 64. Drakoulis now gave up all hope for his own situation. Having no prospect any longer of ruling, he decided to
kill his enemies by making a desperate attack, and to die in
the attempt. Having made this senseless resolve, he decided to
attack the camp by night. So about midnight he took his men
and attacked one corner of the camp, in disorderly fashion and
without any plan. He slaughtered a considerable number of
animals, camels, and horses and mules, but he did not succeed in reaching the men.

§ 65. When the Sultan learned of the attack, he purposely
ordered his soldiers to fall back a little, so as to draw the
enemy farther forward and make him more vulnerable. Then
he gave the army the signal ordering a general attack from
all sides. So they rushed in with a shout and with great dash
and eagerness, and slaughtered all on the spot except a considerable number whom they took alive.

Defeat and flight of Drakoulis

§ 66. Drakoulis hid in a certain place, and then fled and

got away as a fugitive to Paeonia. The Paeonians [Hungarians] arrested him and shut him up in prison. And the Sultan, as I have said, appointed Rados as ruler of the Getae and gave over to him all rule and authority over them, taking pledges from him. Then he recrossed the Ister, taking with him an immense quantity of booty, prisoners, and cattle which he distributed to the army. He reached Adrianople in the fall and gave his army a brief rest there.

Reasons why the Sultan made an expedition against Lesbos and Mitylene

§ 67. After this he summoned the chiefs of the fleet and commanded them to fit out a fleet of two hundred ships against Lesbos. For Nikorezos, the son of Dorieus, who with his brother Dominicus had been left the heir to his father's domains when their father died,[31] and who had made a treaty with the Sultan and was paying tribute, first made a foul plot and acted impiously, and then arrested and imprisoned his own brother and treacherously murdered him.

§ 68. Thereafter he failed to pay the tribute promptly to the Sultan, and was unwilling to be faithful to his treaty obligations, but carried on secret negotiations with the Italians. He made pacts with them and, as I have said, broke his treaty with the Sultan. In many other ways, and in particular by tolerating the visits of pirate ships, by hiring other such men himself, and furnishing them with guides to the towns, and harbors and such places, he clandestinely did damage to the entire coasts of the Sultan opposite Lesbos. Not only this, but he also attacked the Chersonese itself and the coasts of Thrace and Macedonia beyond.

§ 69. The Sultan often heard of this, and sent and ordered him not to act thus, in view of his treaty of peace, for he could not hide such evil deeds. The Sultan admonished him that he must remain faithful to his treaty and pay the tribute without fail, or else he would make war against him.

§ 70. The man denied some of the charges, and thought

[31] Nicolo and Domenico, sons of Dorino of the Gattilusio family.

he could conceal some facts. And as he had some vain hopes of help from the Italians, he paid little attention to the Sultan. So, after threatening him many times, the Sultan sent a fleet, as I stated above, and devastated a part of Lesbos so as to bring him to his senses. But this did not change him. Though for a while he thought best, because he was afraid, to do certain things and to refrain from others, he still remained unchanged.

§ 71. So the Sultan was angered at him and made his expedition against him. He made his preparations as rapidly as possible, got his fleet well armed, placed many heavy infantry and all sorts of weapons on board, including stone-firing cannon and cross-bows, appointed Mahmud Pasha as admiral-in-chief, and sent them off.

Advance of the Sultan against Lesbos by land and sea

§ 72. He himself with his army crossed the Hellespont, marched through Phrygia Minor,[32] and reached Ilium. He observed its ruins and the traces of the ancient city of Troy, its size and position and all the advantages of the country, and its favorable location as to land and sea. He also inquired about the tombs of the heroes—Achilles and Ajax and the rest.

How the Sultan examined the tombs of the heroes, as he passed through Troy, and how he praised and congratulated them

§ 73. And he praised and congratulated them, their memory and their deeds, and on having a person like the poet Homer to extol them. He is reported to have said, shaking his head a little, "God has reserved for me, through so long a period of years, the right to avenge this city and its inhabitants. For I have subdued their enemies and have plundered their cities and made them the spoils of the Mysians. It was the Greeks and Macedonians and Thessalians and Peloponnesians who ravaged this place in the past, and whose descendants have now through my efforts paid the just penalty,

32 Region south of the Marmara and the Dardanelles.

after a long period of years, for their injustice to us Asiatics at that time and so often in subsequent times."

§ 74. So then, starting on from there, he came to Cape Lecton, and going on farther he encamped on the mainland opposite Lesbos and right opposite to Mitylene.

§ 75. And Mahmud, sailing from Gallipoli with the whole fleet of two hundred ships, on the third day arrived at Mitylene and, having disembarked his troops, pitched camp not far from the city. The Mityleneans then first made a sortie, but accomplished nothing and were driven back again by the heavy infantry into the city, where they shut the gates and waited.

Siege of Mitylene

§ 76. Mahmud first addressed them and their commander, asking if they were willing to surrender themselves and their city to the Sultan and to make terms with him. But as he could not persuade them, he first ravaged the country around and devastated everything. Later he built palisades around the city and surrounded it with his army. He set up his cannon against it and laid siege, and within six or seven days at the most he had wrecked a great part of the wall, demolishing it with his cannon.

§ 77. When the inhabitants saw that the wall was wrecked, they brought up great beams, fastened palings in front and behind them, piled up earth and other things inside, and fought from there.

§ 78. The Sultan watched the proceedings from beyond the camp, and decided that he should wait no longer, but should make every preparation for his entire army to attack the city and capture it by a single assault. He immediately ordered the army and all the ammunition to cross over to the island as quickly as possible. And they crossed.

Crossing of the Sultan to Lesbos

§ 79. The Sultan embarked in a trireme and was ferried across to the island. When he had joined Mahmud, he found out all the facts. Then he mounted his horse and examined the city, its vulnerable and invulnerable points by land and sea. And he ordered the entire army to be drawn up, and the triremes to be armed so as to attack by sea from the harbor.

Capture of Mitylene and advance through Lesbos

§ 80. But at this juncture those in the city and their commander, when they saw that the Sultan had crossed over and that the army was ready to attack them by land and sea, feared that they would be captured by assault. They saw that the wall was demolished by the cannon and that the army was immense and strong and fully armed, and also that the attack by the Sultan was irresistible and that he would never leave the island until he had completely subdued it. So they sent a messenger to offer their surrender and that of the city to the Sultan, and also to beg for forgiveness because they had not yielded immediately when summoned.

§ 81. The Sultan received these men and gave them pledges. Accordingly the Mitylenians came out of their city with their commander, made obeisance before the Sultan, and surrendered the city to him. He accepted them generously, and gave them handsome presents. Then he entered the town and looked it over carefully, and it appeared to him very fine and very beautiful. The men from the other fortresses and towns also came and surrendered themselves and those fortresses.

§ 82. After spending four whole days on the island, inspecting it and everything in it and admiring its size and beauty and the various advantages of the country and its arrangement, the Sultan then embarked in a trireme and crossed over to his camp, leaving Mahmud to arrange affairs in the city and throughout the island according to his instructions.

Notes

§ 83. Mahmud gathered all the inhabitants of the city, men, women, and children, and divided them into three parts.

The first part he allowed to stay in the city and inhabit it, retaining and enjoying their own property and paying the customary yearly tribute. The second he deported to Constantinople and settled there. And the third he made slaves and distributed to the soldiers. As many mercenaries of the Italians as he found in the city, he killed every one.

§ 84. As for the other forts and towns in the island, he allowed them temporarily to remain as they were. But later he captured and destroyed some of them, transferring the men and children and women to Constantinople. So Mahmud in this way arranged affairs in Mitylene and in the whole of Lesbos. He installed a considerable garrison in the city and in the other fortresses, and left there a governor, one of the best known of all his men and one exceptionally famed for his courage and strategy and other qualifications, a Samian named Ali. He then went back to the Sultan.

§ 85. The admirals of the fleet took with them the ruler of the Lesbians and all his suite, also the men, children, and women who were destined for repopulating the City. They placed in the ships the immense booty of all sorts, sailed home to Gallipoli and Byzantium, and disbanded the fleet.

§ 86. The Sultan disbanded the army and reached Byzantium with his personal bodyguard at the end of autumn. Thus ended the year 6970, which was the twelfth of the Sultan's reign [A.D. 1462].

§ 87. Thus was Lesbos conquered by the Sultan, and Mitylene too, after it had prospered and enjoyed great glory and power and wealth for 150 years, from the time when Nikorezos, the first of the Gateliouzes family, originally received this island from the Roman Emperor. He was an Italian and a well-born man, very wise and highly educated, rich in moral courage and having other and physical gifts as well. And he knew thoroughly and to the best degree how to administer government. He had brought the island up to such a state, and improved it so in every respect by the gifts and services which little by little he gave to it, that it could vie in nearly every respect with its own ancient prosperity.

§ 88. The island not only subjugated the neighboring and

less remote places, but even the whole of Syria and Egypt feared it and brought annual tribute to it, thus purchasing peace with the holder of the island. For it had and maintained a worthy navy, and had very many triremes, some in use and others in naval arsenals, by means of which it held absolute control not only of the seas around itself but also of those around Egypt and Syria and even Libya.

§ 89. This ruler pillaged and devastated all of those places by piracy, until, when the control of this realm had been passed down from generation to generation and the realm itself had become somewhat less in extent in course of time, the ancestors of the Sultan, and finally the Sultan himself secured the control of the sea round about and subjugated all the places in it, so that this island also, among the rest, became subject to the Sultan and paid tribute. And now it was completely conquered.

§ 90. On his return to Constantinople, the Sultan established the Mitylenians in one quarter of the City. To some he gave houses, to others, land to build houses on, and to still others, whatever else that they needed. Nikorezos, their chief, he then shut up in prison; but shortly afterward he killed him as guilty.

Showing how the Sultan wished to build a great navy, and have control of the sea

§ 91. Then he gave orders that, in addition to the existing ships, a large number of others should speedily be built and many sailors selected from all his domains for this purpose and set aside for this work alone. He did this because he saw that sea-power was a great thing, that the navy of the Italians was large and that they dominated the sea and ruled all the islands in the Aegean, and that to no small extent they injured his own coastlands, both Asiatic and European—especially the navy of the Venetians. Hence he determined to prevent this by every means and to be the powerful master of the entire sea if he could, or at least to prevent them from harming his possessions. For this purpose he got together as quickly as possible a great fleet, and began to gain control of the sea.

§ 92. After this, on thinking it over, he concluded that it would be very wise and indeed of the utmost necessity to ensure his possession of the Strait of the Hellespont and of the Chersonese by very strongly built fortresses on both shores in order to connect the continents of Asia and Europe and to make an enclosed sea out of all the upper sea, that is, the Euxine and the Hellespont, and also to secure this firmly by closing the Strait, so that if enemies attacked, its coasts should not be ravaged—as indeed he had earlier done for the Bosporus.

Showing how the Sultan planned to build two fortresses on the Chersonese, opposite each other, in Asia and Europe, and close the Strait and all the upper sea of the Hellespont and the Pontus

§ 93. Having made this decision, the Sultan immediately sent men to examine the lay of the land and to ascertain the narrowest part and the swiftest current in the Strait. These men went and took measurements. They found that the narrowest and swiftest point of the Strait was the part between Madytus [Maydos] and Eleous [Seddulbahr], toward the opposite point of the continent of Asia, or Dardania [Chanak-kale], as it is called, a width of about eight stadia. There there happened to be the ruins also of an old tower, built by some former king who wanted to close the Strait, it is said, by a chain, but was unable to do so because the strength of the current easily turned and twisted and wound up the chain. So they came back and reported this to the Sultan.

§ 94. As quickly as possible he summoned Yakub, Governor of Gallipoli and the Chersonese, Admiral of the entire fleet, and Commander of the whole shore, and charged him with the building of the forts, to be carried out as promptly as possible, together with all the responsibility for other things in this connection, without slackening speed. This man, without the least hesitation, immediately constructed them with a large force of eager workmen. He spent a large sum of money on the work.

Of the Bostrians [Bosnians], and how the Sultan made an expedition against them

§ 95. That winter the Sultan made his preparations so that in early spring he might march his army against the Paeonians south of the Save River, whom they call Dalmatians, but the moderns call them Bostrians. They are a nation large and numerous with a great kingdom and very much land from which they get good crops and fruits, a land protected by very great natural ruggedness, by well-nigh impassable craggy mountains and steep precipices. Further, this land has strong fortresses and well fortified towns hard to capture. It also has wealthy and powerful chiefs. Besides this, they have eternal friendship and alliance with the king of the Paeonians [Hungarians] and treaties and strict promises that if one party is attacked, the other party will help them.

§ 96. Trusting in all this, they were never willing to make a treaty with the Sultan or to pay him an annual tribute as did other frontier peoples like the Illyrians and the Triballi, or to be in any form subject to him. On the contrary, although the Sultan had invited them many times to make a treaty, they had disdained it, and would not agree to such a step, preferring to be free and independent and not bound by any treaty.

§ 97. For this reason the Sultan had often sent in an army to plunder their country, overrunning it and carrying away great quantities of plunder, and men, children, women and flocks. But still they would not stir from their former position. They kept to the beliefs they had once adopted, even to their own disaster.

§ 98. Angered at this, the Sultan made an expedition against them. He made careful preparation, gathered many arms and a variety of cannon plus an immense army of horse and foot. And just at the opening of spring he set out against them with a strong and numerous force.

Movement of the Sultan against the Bostrians. Overrunning of their country

§ 99. So then, starting from Adrianople with his entire army, horse and foot, by continuous and rapid marches he soon traversed his own territory and, when he reached the boundaries of the Bostrians, encamped there a short time. After that he attacked their country vigorously and overran it, falling on it like a thunderbolt, burning, ruining, and destroying everything. He captured fortresses, in some of which he placed garrisons, and took away booty. And he subdued the whole country, for no one was able to resist.

§ 100. Finally, after he had marched through most of the country in a short period of days, and overrun it and captured many fortresses and towns, some, as I said, by assault and armed force and others by surrender, he reached the town where their chief had taken refuge.

Arrival of the Sultan at Yaitsa, and its siege

§ 101. This town was very strongly fortified. It was called in the local tongue Yaitsa. He besieged the chief here, and also began negotiations with the townspeople for the surrender of themselves and the place. But, as he could not persuade them, he built ramparts around the city, surrounded it with his army, placed the cannon in position, and laid siege to it. He demolished a large part of the wall with his cannon in a few days, and laid it low. Then he made preparations to assault it with his whole army.

§ 102. The people in the town saw that most of the wall was destroyed and that the Sultan was about to make a massed assault. Therefore, fearing that if it were taken by attack they would be destroyed, they sent secret messengers to the Sultan, without the knowledge of their chief, and surrendered themselves and the town. But the chief, on hearing of this, left the town secretly and fled.

§ 103. However the sentinels of the besieging force got wind of this, pursued hotly after him, captured him alive, and brought him to the Sultan, who immediately had him executed. Then the townspeople went out and gave up themselves and the town to the Sultan.

§ 104. He received them kindly and gave them many sorts of presents, allowing them to live in the city, safely and unharmed, with their wives and children and all their possessions, simply on the customary condition of paying an annual tribute. After that he himself entered the city, and looked it over carefully. It impressed him as being very strong. He decided it must be preserved and garrisoned, and that it would serve his purpose well.

Destruction of all the country of the Bostrians, and capture of all the towns in it, nearly 300

§ 105. This was because it lies in a suitable part of the country, on the boundary of the Paeonians, and can accommodate a considerable garrison which could do much harm to the latter. For that reason the Sultan considered its possession of the highest importance. Accordingly, he left a sufficient garrison there, with one of his own household as commandant. Then he, at the head of the army, went against the rest of the country. Before the summer had entirely passed, he had ravaged all the land of the Bostrians and the Dalmatians, and pillaged it, and captured a little less than three hundred castles. He also made prisoner four of their chiefs.

Reasons why the Venetians broke their treaty with the Sultan, and fought with him

§ 106. That same summer, the Venetians broke their treaty with the Sultan, and declared war on him, alleging the following accusations as reasons: Omer, governor-general of the Peloponnesus and of the rest of Greece, moving on very little provocation, or indeed without any provocation, being simply angered by the fact that the Venetians showed him no friendship or kindness even though he was a neighboring governor who could do them harm, considered himself slighted by them and sought to wreak vengeance on them. Therefore, awaiting the favorable moment, he made an unexpected at-

tack on the people of Naupactus [Lepanto], overran Naupactus and its environs, and carried off as spoils many men,
animals, children, and women. He had fallen on them suddenly and was utterly unexpected, nor did they foresee anything, in a time of peace when they had treaties. Hence he
did them great harm, and even came very near capturing the
town of Naupactus itself.

§ 107. Not only that, but he also maltreated the Venetians'
towns of Coroneia and Methone in the Peloponnesus, and
others, offering in each case empty pretexts as reason. This
was very hard for the Venetians to bear, and was the greatest
cause for their going to war. In addition they had been aching
for war with the Sultan ever since he had conquered the
Peloponnesus, for they had always counted on having it for
themselves. Therefore, believing they had lost what was really
their own, they waited for the suitable time and pretext for
declaring war on the Sultan and for marching against his
country.

Expedition of the Venetians against the Peloponnesus

§ 108. Hence they seized upon these pretexts immediately.
And, without sending any embassy whatsoever or trying to
solve their difficulties by negotiation, they got together a large
army and a sea-going fleet for the Peloponnesus. It was composed of seventy triremes and large galleons. These they filled
with crews. They embarked in them as many heavy infantry
as they could, and soldiers with coats of mail, ready for battle,
from their own recruits and classes, but with hired mercenaries as well, in great numbers. They also loaded into the
ships arms of all sorts, and stone-shooting cannon and crossbows; also iron in large quantities, and wood, and lime. Added
to these were technicians and builders, and material for building. They also loaded and stowed carefully away much else
for all sorts of uses. And they appointed as commander-in-
chief one of their most experienced men, well known for his
bravery and military skill both on land and sea. Thus they
despatched the fleet.

§ 109. So, setting sail from their city with a great force and after every sort of preparation, with a notable army and with brilliant hopes, they sailed through the Adriatic and Ionian seas. Then, sailing by Corcyra and Leucas, between the adjacent islands of Ithaca and Cephallenia, they headed for Elis, in the extreme west of the Peloponnesus. Thence they went along the coast of Achaia and, passing through the Crissaean [Gulf of Corinth], arrived at Corinth on the Isthmus.

Relating how the Venetians built a wall at the Isthmus of the Peloponnesus

§ 110. There they disembarked and encamped. They intended to build a wall there and get possession of this town first, and then later to capture the whole of the Peloponnesus. So they unloaded all the cargo and everything they needed, and occupied the Isthmus from coast to coast with all their army. They built the wall using many workmen and great energy and all haste and eagerness.

§ 111. At that time some of the fortresses and towns belonging to the Sultan revolted, both in the inland and on the shores, and joined the Italians who established garrisons in them. Not only this, but all the rest of the Peloponnesus was in doubt and watching to see what would happen, so as to be able also to revolt from the Sultan.

§ 112. Omer collected all of his troops and added to them some of the Illyrians [Albanians] from the Peloponnesus, thus forming a rather numerous army. He himself stayed at Corinth, guarding the city and waiting for an army to be sent from the Sultan. He had already sent a messenger to him, as soon as the fleet started, warning him of the coming attack. At the same time he watched for a good opportunity to attack the Venetians.

How the Sultan sent Mahmud to the Peloponnesus with an army against the Venetians

§ 113. When the Sultan heard of the expedition of the

Venetians against the Peloponnesus and of their building a wall across the Isthmus, he decided not to delay any longer. Therefore he quickly called Mahmud Pasha and gave him a large army of heavy infantry and bowmen and of soldiers from his own bodyguard, the best fighters and the best armed. And he sent him to the Peloponnesus.

§ 114. Therefore Mahmud put in good order all his affairs among the Bostrians, according to his previous plan, and placed garrisons and commanders in Yaitsa and the other fortresses which he had not destroyed. He left in that region a considerable army and a governor—a man he knew well to be brave and of military ability. Then, having taken a large quantity of booty, he went back to Adrianople, as the autumn was at its close. This was the end of the year 6971 in all [A.D. 1463], which was the thirteenth year of the reign of the Sultan.

PART V

S U M M A R Y

Including the war with the Venetians and the second expedition of the Sultan against the Bostrians; also the first and second expeditions of the Sultan against the Illyrians, and how he subdued their country and fortified a city in it. Period covered: four years [A.D. 1464-1467].

[Of Mahmud's arrival]

§ 1. On his arrival in the Peloponnesus, Mahmud encamped on the outer side of the Isthmus on the slopes of Mount Kithaeron. And, sending a secret messenger, he communicated to Omer the news of his arrival with an army. He asked for information as to all the affairs at the Isthmus and all about the enemy. And then, having agreed as to the attack to be launched on a given day, they rested.

§ 2. The Venetians, in great haste and zeal, and by employing a large force of men for the work on the wall, completed it quickly. Indeed, they had already finished the whole wall except for three or four stadia, though they had not raised it as high as was desired, but merely enough to defend themselves safely.

Clash of Mahmud with the Venetians on the Isthmus; defeat of the Venetians and their flight and slaughter

§ 3. At this time Omer, watching for the moment to attack, gave the signal to Mahmud and with perfect timing they both rushed in and attacked the enemy's camp, the one from the inner side and the other from without, with a shout and a loud noise made by the soldiers shouting their battle-cries.

§ 4. Then there was great struggling and pushing and a fierce hand-to-hand battle and much slaughter. For a short time, on receiving the onslaught of the heavy infantry, the Venetians resisted. But then they broke and fled precipitately in disorder and with no discipline.

§ 5. The heavy infantry followed on, killing them mercilessly or taking them prisoner, till they reached the sea and their ships. There, by great effort, the Venetians managed to board their ships and put off a little from the shore, getting a breathing space when out of range of the arrows. Then they took on board those that had swum out to them, for many had been so hard pressed by their attackers that they threw away their arms and cast themselves into the sea. Others swam off carrying their arms, and some reached the ships while others were drowned under the weight of their weapons.

Plunder of the Venetian camp

§ 6. There fell in the battle a large number of the Venetians, both of the men of the city and foreigners. Among them was the general himself, who was a noble man. A little less than three hundred were taken prisoner. The soldiers plundered the whole camp, where they found much money plus furnishings and drinking-cups besides many supplies and other necessary things. Many weapons were also captured, some of them stripped from the slain, and others in warehouses. There were also many cannon of all sorts, and other such things.

§ 7. After this, Mahmud resumed his march. He went into the interior of the Peloponnesus, with Omer, against the fortresses that were resisting and against the rest of the Peloponnesians that had revolted. Within a few days they captured the fortresses and all other places, some by assault, while others were persuaded to surrender.

§ 8. After that he reached Argos, a town of the Venetians, and encamped before the city. He addressed the inhabitants, advising them to surrender themselves and the town. Thereupon the Argives, seeing the great size of the army surrounding the city, and knowing that their wall was weak and quite vulnerable and that there was no rescue from anywhere, nor even a hope of any, and also fearing lest in the event of an attack they might be overcome by military force and be destroyed, surrendered themselves and their city to Mahmud without a fight, after being given pledges.

Surrender of Argos to Mahmud, and transfer of the Argives to Byzantium, and destruction of Argos

§ 9. He colonized all of them in Byzantium, with their wives and children and all their belongings, safe and unhurt, but the city he razed to the ground. Then he arranged everything in the Peloponnesus in good shape, according to his plan. He left guards in every fortress, the most warlike of the men of the royal guard, and he put in good order everything that had been disarranged by the uprising. Then he turned over everything to Omer while he himself took with him the men captured on the Isthmus and those Venetians whom he had found in the fortresses. He also took those of the Peloponnesians who had revolted and a small amount of booty, and returned to Constantinople, for it was already midwinter.

§ 10. The Sultan settled all the Argives in the monastery of Peribleptos, giving them also houses and vineyards and fields. But he killed all the Venetian prisoners, whom I mentioned as taken in the fortresses, and also the Peloponnesians who had revolted.

How the forts at the Hellespont were completed by Yakub, and armed well, and the straits closed

§ 11. During that same period the Governor of Gallipoli, Yakub, completed the forts at the Hellespont and placed a garrison in them, brought in a great quantity of arms, and set up stone-shooting cannon and crossbows, with the intention of stopping the ingress and egress of ships sailing up or down, whenever and however he chose. He also carried out all the other orders of the Sultan.

§ 12. Thus was brought to completion a great and complicated task, worthy of all praise and admiration, a task which no one of the ancient Greeks nor of the great kings and generals of old—that is, among Romans and Persians—had ever thought of or could have thought of: namely, to separate the upper sea [Black] from the lower [Aegean], and to prevent completely and make entirely impossible the navigation up or down for any who might wish it, except for those whom he himself was willing to allow to pass. He did this by placing the fortresses like gates on either side and by planting stone-shooting cannon. For fear of these triremes and the largest galleons alike kept at a respectful distance, as did everything else, even large or small rowboats. For as soon as ships approached they were immediately sunk and demolished by the immense stone balls fired from the cannon, as if they were caught between Scylla and Charybdis.

§ 13. Xerxes, it is true, of old had bridged this Hellespont by rafts and a wooden bridge. But this could not stand long against the assaults of wind and wave, nor did it stand, in fact. This was because a hostile power coming against it could easily break it up by force.

§ 14. But in the present case, nothing of that sort is happening or can happen. Neither the assaults and blows of the sea, nor the winds, nor the attacks of enemy armies can totally destroy this, or force it in any way, so impregnable and strong is this new fetter and obstacle.

How the King of the Paeonians attacked Yaitsa after the Sultan's departure, and captured it by treachery, the inhabitants surrendering it, and how he took some other forts in the same way

§ 15. During the same winter the King of the Paeonians and Dacians[33] attacked Dalmatia and the country of the Bostrians, which formerly the Sultan had held, to see if possibly he might capture it and hold the fortresses there, especially Yaitsa, after driving out the Sultan's garrison. He considered it the worst possible thing, a very great detriment and an evident threat of destruction to his own country, that this region and the forts in it should be held by the Sultan, since it was advantageously situated against him. It bordered on the territory of the Paeonians all the way, and was suitable for incursions into that country.

§ 16. So he attacked it with a large and well equipped army, and quickly captured most of the forts from the Sultan,

---

[33] Mathias Corvinus of Hungary.

some on terms of surrender, others by terrorism and threats, and a few by armed force. Then he came to Yaitsa and took it without a struggle, for rebellion broke out inside and the garrison slew one another. Hence the survivors willingly surrendered.

§ 17. After spending a few days there, he left a strong garrison of well-armed and warlike men in the city and in the other fortresses, supplying them with large quantities of arms and troops and provisions, and then left for home.

§ 18. When the Sultan learned this, he was deeply moved by what he heard, and immediately prepared to set out against the region with a large and powerful army, not only against the country of the Bostrians and the surrendered fortresses, but also to invade the land of the Paeonians. So he raised a very large army of both cavalry and infantry, and gathered many weapons and stone-shooting cannon and crossbows. He also made careful preparation along all lines throughout the winter. And on the arrival of spring he set out against them.

Second expedition of the Sultan against Paeonia and the Bostrians

§ 19. Leaving Adrianople with all his army, horse and foot, and taking along with him the cannon and a great quantity of copper and iron, he went against the country of the Bostrians. On reaching there he realized he must first go against Yaitsa and capture it if he could, either by persuasion or by armed force, and then go for other places.

Second Siege of Yaitsa

§ 20. So he marched against it and pitched his camp before the city. First he made overtures to the forces inside, to surrender themselves and the city, he giving them guarantees. But as they did not accept, he first devastated and burned the whole region around it. Then he dug a trench before the city, surrounded it with his army, set up the cannon, and laid siege. And for a few days he battered the wall with his cannon and made breaches in it.

199

First attack of the Sultan on Yaitsa,
and its failure

§ 21. As soon as he thought a wide enough breach had been made, he prepared to attack the wall with his full force and might. Therefore he arranged and armed the soldiers, and attacked from all sides. He himself took command at the point where the wall had been destroyed, and with him his bodyguard and the very pick of the army, including heavy infantry, bowmen, slingers, and especially musketeers. As soon as they heard the signal, the soldiers gave a mighty and terrifying shout, and with a strong and swift assault made their way against the wrecked part of the wall and tried to climb it by force.

§ 22. But the Paeonians responded very bravely and stoutly, with an outlandish hue and cry. There followed a fierce hand-to-hand battle and a great struggle, much charging and mingled shouting on both sides, and swearing and no little slaughter of brave men. Those on the one side were trying to force their way through and capture the town; those on the other to repulse them and to guard their possessions, that is, their children and wives and their most valuable goods. Sometimes the heavy infantry would force the Paeonians back, and win out and scale the wall. At other, they would again be driven back by the Paeonians and repulsed by superior force, and many of them would fall fighting, and die.

§ 23. This went on for quite a long time, both sides fighting bravely. Then the Paeonians proved much more successful; and the heavy infantry were pressed back and suffered terribly, many fine brave men among them falling there. So the Sultan was very much troubled at seeing his men so terribly battered and destroyed, and he gave the signal for retreat, and ordered them out of bowshot. And they withdrew.

Second unsuccessful attack

§ 24. Again not many days after this, after resting his army and rearming and rearranging it in good order, he made a vigorous assault on the town, he himself being at the very front. And he offered rewards, and added to these very many and very large sums, with many honors and privileges, to those who would first scale the walls. He also gave permission to plunder and rob all the people in the city.

§ 25. The soldiers, with a great and fearful battle-cry, immediately flew at the wall like birds of prey, with great force and rush, but in disorder and without keeping ranks or discipline, and tried to climb it. Some placed ladders against it, others suspended ropes, others fastened stakes or pegs in the wall, while still others tried in every possible way to break through. For the Sultan was present and watched the feats and the onslaught and zeal and bravery and energy and discipline of each one, and they had the greatest expectation of prizes, hoping to receive no small reward. Each one wanted to be the first to climb the wall, or to kill a Paeonian, or to plant the standard on the wall or battlements.

Noting the severe battle

§ 26. The Paeonians replied most energetically, and with very great daring and élan and swiftness, with a great shout, and met their enemy bravely and stoutly. A fierce and terrible battle took place there, such as no one ever saw or heard of in a fight at the walls; especially around the point at which the wall had been breached. For, drunken with battle, they yielded entirely to anger and wrath, well-nigh ignoring nature itself. They slaughtered each other and mercilessly cut each other to pieces, charging and being charged, wounding and being wounded, killing and being killed, shouting, blaspheming, swearing, hardly conscious of anything that was happening or of what they were doing, just like madmen.

§ 27. Thus many fine heroes fell, of the heavy infantry and especially of those in the royal guard, prodigal of themselves, and ashamed to do any less while before the very eyes of the Sultan, for he was fighting by their side. But the Paeonians prevailed generally everywhere, for they were fighting from higher ground and attacking from a vantage-point and were stronger in their efforts. For they were all fine warriors, selected for their valor.

§ 28. The Sultan saw that his men were being sadly depleted, and that the struggle was not going well anywhere, but that it had been proven well-nigh impossible to capture the city by assault, and also that this could be done only by starving them out by means of a long siege. Accordingly he gave the order to move back, and the army withdrew out of range of the arrows.

§ 29. Withdrawing, then, to the camp, the Sultan arranged to leave behind at the city a considerable army to besiege it and prevent any from escaping from within or entering from without. He, himself, with the balance of the army, went into the rest of the country, against the revolted fortresses, but especially against the Paeonians.

March of the Paeonian [Hungarian] King against the Sultan

§ 30. Just at this moment came news to the effect that the king of the Paeonians had raised an unprecedentedly large army and was marching against him. For this king, as soon as he knew that the Sultan had invaded the Bostrian country, and learned about the siege of the city of Yaitsa, collected a large army, prepared great quantities of whatever he could get, and started out against the Sultan, thinking that thus he would either raise the siege of the city by turning the Sultan and his army against himself, or else he would split the army into two forces, one for the fighting and the other for the siege, and so would have the advantage of a fight with a weakened Sultan. But he was mistaken in his idea.

§ 31. For the Sultan, when he learned this, felt he must remain at Yaitsa and continue the siege, and not leave the place. But he sent off Mahmud against the king of the Paeonians, giving him a considerable force of foot and horse, and no small portion of his own bodyguard.

§ 32. He did not believe he ought to go in person to fight against this man. Therefore Mahmud took the army and went by forced marches. When he had come very near the enemy, he encamped there. Between the two camps not over twenty-five stadia intervened at most, so that they could see each other. The Erygon River ran between, dividing them from each other, a stream called in the local language Vrynos. Here, on the far side of the river, the king of the Paeonians had encamped.

§ 33. Now Mahmud was planning to cross the river and attack the Paeonians. But the Sultan sent and stopped him, saying there was no need, for the present at least, of crossing the river, but it was enough to stay right there and watch the movements of the enemy. Mahmud remained there and rested, and kept watch on the enemy.

§ 34. The leader of the Paeonians, when he learned that the Sultan was still besieging the city and had no idea of abandoning it, and that Mahmud with a big army was waiting for him, gave up all hope of being able effectively to help the city, and secretly sent a messenger to tell those inside the city to resist, and never to surrender. He added that the Sultan would soon be withdrawing again, and that he himself would not lose sight of him, but that when the occasion called for it and an urgent need arose, he would help them all he could, since he would be close at hand.

Retreat of the Paeonian King, and disorderly and disgraceful rout, with Mahmud in pursuit

§ 35. Then he burned his camp by night, and went off in haste with his army. As soon as Mahmud learned this, he swiftly crossed the river, and marched in hot pursuit. Catching up with them, he fell upon the rearguard, a fairly large body detailed to guard the baggage train, and drove them back on to the main army.

§ 36. So they came on them suddenly, and set both army and king in confusion. Thereby the flight became a rout, all fleeing together in disorder, with no semblance of keeping ranks or of plan.

§ 37. Mahmud followed on, killing and slaughtering them mercilessly. And after driving them a long way, and making a great slaughter, and capturing many alive, he returned and came to the Sultan, bringing all their equipment, carts, arms, horses, and the baggage-carriers themselves. Very many of the enemy were killed. Those captured alive were a little short of two hundred. Later the Sultan brought them to Byzantium and executed them all.

§ 38. After continuing the siege a few days and unsuccessfully trying several methods for capturing the town, he abandoned the attempt and withdrew his army. Instead he turned to the other fortified places, and in a short time had secured possession of them. In some of them he placed strong garrisons, where it seemed best to him, while others he demolished, killing the men and enslaving the women and children. He also pillaged most of the rest of the country, and also no small part of that of the Paeonians. Carrying off for himself an enormous amount of booty, and distributing part of his army, he left a governor in charge of the region. Then, since the summer was now ending, he went back to Constantinople and disbanded his army.

Expeditions of the Venetians against Lesbos, with seventy ships

§ 39. That same summer the Venetians made an expedition against Lesbos and Mitylene in seventy triremes and large galleons and with three thousand heavy infantry whom they had on the decks. They also carried in the galleons many weapons, and stone-hurling cannon and crossbows and scaling-ladders, and all other equipment for fighting against walls. On arriving at Lesbos, they anchored in the harbor of Mitylene, landed and pitched camp before the city, and opened negotiations with the citizens as to surrendering themselves and their city. But these rejected the proposal, for there were in the town four hundred picked men from the Sultan's bodyguard, heavily armored.

§ 40. Then first the Venetians stripped only a part of the land, for they did not want to devastate it all, as they hoped to get possession of it. After this they surrounded the entire city, on the land side by their army and by sea with the ships. They set up the cannon and began the siege, and they damaged a small part of the wall in a few days with their cannon, and knocked it down. But the men in the city repaired it again by night, bringing up stones and wood and earth. Besides this, they brought great beams and made palisades about the wall, and some of the beams they suspended with chains, thus breaking the force of the stone cannon-balls or else deflecting them, so that these stones did no great damage.

§ 41. There were skirmishes and sorties every day, and the imperial troops sallied forth against the Venetians. However, none were killed, only they wounded many of them. The besiegers also dug under the wall, making mines toward the city. They also brought up ladders, and used all sorts of siege engines.

§ 42. Two of the other towns also surrendered to them, so that they had the highest hopes of capturing Mitylene and of overcoming and conquering the whole of Lesbos.

Sailing of the Sultan's fleet against that of the Venetians' at Lesbos

§ 43. This was the situation. Then the Sultan, hearing of the attack of the Venetian fleet against Mitylene, and of its siege, and how it was in danger of being taken by the Venetians unless relieved immediately, armed one hundred and ten triremes right off, quicker than you could say so, and put aboard a very large number of heavy infantry and all sorts of powerful weapons and all necessary things. Having equipped them well, he confided the fleet to Mahmud Pasha, ordering him to sail at top speed and attack the enemy's ships wherever they happened to be.

Capture of two scouting ships of the Venetians at Tenedos

§ 44. So Mahmud set sail from Byzantium and made for the Hellespont, and reached Gallipoli the second day after. Here he learned that four enemy scout triremes were anchored in Tenedos harbor, that they had sailed up as far as the mouth of the Straits to explore, and had gone back again. Without delay he sailed immediately by night from Gallipoli with the entire fleet, so that he might not be seen or suspected. Taking advantage of favorable winds, he reached Tenedos at daybreak, and surprised the triremes anchored in the harbor. Two of them he captured with all their men, at the entrance of the harbor, for they did not succeed in eluding him.

Precipitate flight of the Venetian fleet from Lesbos on hearing of the approach of the Sultan's fleet against them

§ 45. The other two had sailed earlier. They barely escaped, for they were the fastest sort of sailers and, making all speed, they reached Mitylene and announced to the generals the coming of the Sultan's fleet and the capture of the two ships. On hearing this, they were thunderstruck at the news. Leaving behind everything—cannon and arms and all their other equipment—they embarked in disorder on the triremes without any plan or regularity, taking with them the men, women and children of the fortresses that had surrendered to them, and they got away to sea before the Sultan's fleet could reach Mitylene, by the space, it is stated of about eight hours.

§ 46. On his arrival at Mitylene, Mahmud learned that they had sailed a short time before. He swiftly gave chase, but gained the open sea barely in time to see them making all sail for Lemnos. So he gave up the pursuit and went back to Mitylene, where he spent four days. He arranged everything in good order, and left a sufficient garrison, with weapons and much food and other provisions for the needs of the city, and returned to Byzantium, for the autumn was already passing. And there he disbanded the fleet. So ended the 6972nd year in all, being the fourteenth year of the reign of the Sultan [A.D. 1464].

A Fearful Event

§ 47. During those days a marvelous prodigy appeared. The sun, at high noon, while shining brilliantly and unclouded, was all at once changed, darkened, and obscured.

Its appearance was like dark copper, and it became all dusky and black, but not like its usual appearance in times of eclipse, for there was no eclipse then, but this happened in some different and very new way, as if a mist or a dark foggy cloud had rolled over and covered it up. This lasted three whole days and nights, so that it was observed by everybody. This great and God-given sign showed to everyone that great disasters were to happen in the near future. And these, in point of fact, followed shortly after.

How the Sultan's Palace was completed

§ 48. The Sultan spent the winter in Byzantium. Among other things he attended to the populating and rebuilding and beautifying of the whole City. In particular he completed the palace—a very beautiful structure. Both as to view and as to enjoyment as well as in its construction and its charm, it was in no respect lacking as compared with the famous and magnificent old buildings and sights.

§ 49. In it he had towers built of unusual height and beauty and grandeur, and apartments for men and others for women, and bedrooms and lounging-rooms and sleeping quarters, and very many other fine rooms. There were also various out-buildings and vestibules and halls and porticoes and gateways and porches, and bakeshops and baths of notable design.

§ 50. There was a grand enclosure containing all this. They were all built, as I said, with a view to variety, beauty, size, and magnificence, shining and scintillating with an abundance of gold and silver, within and without and with precious stones and marbles, with various ornaments and colors, all applied with a brilliance and smoothness and lightness most attractive and worked out with the finest and most complete skill, most ambitiously. Both in sculpture and in plastic work, as well as in painting, they were the finest and best of all. Moreover, all parts were most carefully covered and roofed over with a great quantity of very thick lead roofing. And the whole was beautified and adorned with myriads of other brilliant and graceful articles.

§ 51. Not only this, but around the palace were constructed very large and lovely gardens abounding in various sorts of plants and trees, producing beautiful fruit. And there were abundant supplies of water flowing everywhere, cold and clear and drinkable, and conspicuous and beautiful groves and meadows. Besides that, there were flocks of birds, both domesticated fowls and song-birds, twittering and chattering all around, and many sorts of animals, tame and wild, feeding there. Also there were many other fine ornaments and embellishments of various sorts, such as he thought would bring beauty and pleasure and happiness and enjoyment. The Sultan worked all this out with magnificence and profusion.

§ 52. So then, after spending the winter in this palace, when spring began to appear the Sultan resolved on an expedition and made preparations for it. But, as he perceived that the soldiers, even including his own bodyguard, were complaining, and felt abused and annoyed, especially because of the frequent long journeys and expeditions and because they were constantly kept on troublesome trips abroad, and since they said that they had lost everything, both their physical health and their money, their horses and donkeys, and were ruined and suffering in every way, he postponed the start.

How the Sultan gave many kinds of presents to the army

§ 53. Besides, the Sultan himself was greatly exhausted and worn out in body and mind by his continuous and unremitting planning and care and indefatigable labors and dangers and trials, and he needed a time of respite and recuperation. For this reason he knew he ought to remain at home and rest himself and his army during the approaching summer, so that he could have his troops fresher and more enthusiastic for the other undertakings which were ahead. Since he felt so, he disbanded most of the army, giving them presents of many sorts: to some, horses, to others, garments, to others, money, and to still others, other kinds of presents.

§ 54. But the men of his own bodyguard, whom he knew to be diligent, fond of danger, eager and useful in every way, and brave men, he honored with appropriate honors and positions and magnificent gifts, and many other fine things, advancing them and promoting them in rank for their valor.

§ 55. So, having honored them thus, and given them many gifts, as I have indicated, he then disbanded them. He himself spent the summer in Byzantium; but, as his custom was, he did not neglect his efforts for the City, that is, for its populace, giving diligent care to buildings and improvements. He also occupied himself with philosophy, such as that of the Arabs and Persians and Greeks, especially that translated into Arabic. He associated daily with the leaders and teachers among these, and had not a few of them around him and conversed with them. He held philosophical discussions with them about the principles of philosophy, particularly those of the Peripatetics and the Stoics.

How, at the command of the Sultan, the philosopher
George combined into one chart all the description
of the earth in the outlines of Ptolemy

§ 56. He also ran across, somewhere, the charts of Ptolemy, in which he set forth scientifically and philosophically the entire description and outline of the earth. But he wanted to have these, scattered as they were in the various parts of the work, and for that reason hard to understand, brought together into one united whole as a single picture or representation, and thus made clearer and more comprehensible, so as to be more easily understood by the mind, and grasped and well apprehended, for this lesson seemed to him very necessary and most important.

§ 57. So he called for the philosopher George,[34] and put before him the burden of this plan, with the promise of royal reward and honor. And this man gladly agreed to do the work, and carried out with enthusiasm the proposal and command of the Sultan. He took the book in hand with joy, and read it and studied it all summer. By considerable in-

[34] George Amiroukis. See above, Part IV, section 54.

'estigation and by analyzing its wisdom, he wrote out most
atisfactorily and skillfully the whole story of the inhabited
arth in one representation as a connected whole—of the land
nd sea, the rivers, harbors, islands, mountains, cities and
ll, in plain language, giving in this the rules as to measure-
nents of distances and all other essential things. He in-
:tructed the Sultan in the method most necessary and suit-
ible for students and those fond of investigation and of what
is useful.

§ 58. He also put down on the chart the names of the
countries and places and cities, writing them in Arabic, using
as an interpreter his son, who was expert in the languages of
the Arabs and of the Greeks. The Sultan was much delighted
with this work, and admired the wisdom and ingenuity of
Ptolemy, and still more that of the man who had so well exhibited this to him. He rewarded him in many ways and with
many honors.

§ 59. He also ordered him to issue the entire book in
Arabic, and promised him large pay and gifts for this work.

§ 60. While the Sultan busied himself and was occupied
with this and similar studies, the whole summer passed, and
the autumn; and so was ended the 6973rd year in all, being
the fifteenth of the Sultan's reign [A.D. 1465].

Causes which led the Sultan to undertake a campaign against the Illyrians [Albanians]

§ 61. During the whole of that current year the Sultan
and his troops had a good rest; and he was getting ready all
winter for an early start in spring on a campaign against
the Illyrian country. For the Illyrians, as I have previously
said, lived by the Ionian Sea, and for ages had dwelt in
great and very lofty mountains, and had strongly fortified
and impregnable fortresses, both inland and on the coast,
and places that were difficult of access in very broken country, and fortified on all sides and very safe. Trusting to these,
:hey were determined to be autonomous and free in every
vay, and were unwilling to pay a yearly tax, as did all their
eighbors, or to furnish troops for expeditions, either to the

Sultan's father or to this Sultan himself, or to obey him at all.

§ 62. Not only this, but they often impudently crossed their frontiers, with their ruler, and recklessly overran and pillaged the neighboring domains of the Sultan.

§ 63. Both the Sultan himself and his father before him had indeed made expeditions previously against this people, and had overrun their whole country, and devastated it and plundered it and destroyed fortresses, and had taken away many flocks and slaves and very great booty. And at the time, seeing their land devastated and ruined by such incursion, they had yielded and made a treaty for the time being. But after a while they again shamelessly robbed the Sultan's territory and did mischief. They did so because they had the mountains and the inaccessible parts of the country as a refuge and a protection.

§ 64. Inasmuch as there were but one or two passes through the mountains into the country, they guarded these with strong garrisons, and kept their land inviolate from their enemies, and free from injury, unless a large force should invade it and forcibly occupy the mountains and the passes, and so open a door into the whole country. And this was just what the Sultan intended to do, and he did it well.

Start of the Sultan against the Illyrians

§ 65. So, having, as I said, prepared all winter, as he would have to, when spring came he started out against them with a large force, an army of horse and foot, taking along also cannon and arms. He also prepared for building, by taking masons and carpenters, and tools for both those trades, and much iron and copper, and many such things for making walls and fortifications.

Attack of the Sultan on the passes; the battle and the victory, and the holding of the passes

§ 66. So he set out from Adrianople with his entire army of cavalry and infantry, and went swiftly through his own territory. After crossing it at top speed, he arrived at the frontiers of the Illyrians. Here he encamped one day. The next day at dawn he took the light troops, the bowmen and slingers and spearmen, and those with light shields, and attacked the passes which were strongly guarded by the Illyrians. There followed a great hand-to-hand battle, with attack and counter-attack, a terrible struggle, for the Illyrians resisted stoutly and fought bravely. But he routed them and took the passes by force, and drove them out with great slaughter.

§ 67. After that he placed strong guards at the passes, so that those who passed in and out should not be injured by the Illyrian plunderers. Then he ordered the woodcutters and part of the infantry to go in and fell trees and clear away the bushes and thickets and impenetrable tangles, and to level and repair the rough and uneven and altogether impassable roads, and make them wide and smooth for the whole army, horse and foot, and for the pack animals and wagons and other means of transport.

Overrunning of the entire Illyrian country, and its total devastation

§ 68. He himself with the whole army moved in first into their lower lands, the plains, where cavalry could act. This region he entirely overran and plundered. After that he pitched camp at successive points, and advanced, devastating the country, burning the crops or else gathering them in for himself, and destroying and annihilating.

§ 69. And the Illyrians took their children, wives, flocks, and every other movable up into the high and inaccessible mountain fastnesses. They had their arms also, and they settled down to defend themselves in those difficult strongholds and passes against any attackers.

The attack by the army, the fight, and the climbing of the mountains

§ 70. When the Sultan had pillaged and devastated all

their lowlands, he made careful preparations, and after putting the whole army in first-rate condition, moved against the mountains and their passes, and the fortifications in the hills, against the Illyrians and their children and wives and all their belongings. He placed in the van the bowmen and musketeers and slingers, telling them to shoot and fire their arrows and sling their stones against the Illyrians and drive them as far away as possible, and get rid of them by firing at the heights.

§ 71. Behind them he ordered the light infantry, the spearmen, and those with the small shields to go up, and, following them, all the heavy-armed units. These went up slowly and in irregular ranks, up to a certain point, gradually pushing the Illyrians up to the heights. Then with a mighty shout, the light infantry, the heavy infantry, and the spearmen charged the Illyrians, and having put them to flight, they pursued with all their might, and overtook and killed them. And some they captured alive. But some of them, hard pressed by the heavy infantry, hurled themselves from the precipices and crags, and were destroyed.

The Massacre of the Illyrians

§ 72. The heavy and light infantry, and in fact the whole army, scattering over the mountains and the rough country and the ravines, hunted out and made prisoners of the children and women of the Illyrians, and plundered all their belongings. Not only this, but they carried off a very large number of flocks and herds. They scoured thoroughly the whole mountain, and hunted out and secured a very enormous booty of prisoners and cattle and other things, and brought it all down to the camp.

§ 73. A very great number of the Illyrians lost their lives, some in the fighting, and others were executed after being captured, for so the Sultan ordered. And there were captured in those mountains about twenty thousand children, and women, and men.

§ 74. Of the rest of the Illyrians, some were in the fortresses, and some in other mountain ranges where they had fled with their leader, Alexander.[35]

§ 75. There was a fortress there belonging to the Illyrians, in every respect impregnable and very strong, called Kroues [Kroja], which served as an acropolis and gaurd-house for the whole region. The Sultan's father had previously tried in many ways to capture this, by muskets and stone-throwing cannon, and by a long siege, but he had not succeeded in taking it, so impregnable was it.

Abandoning the Attack on Kroues

§ 76. So then, the Sultan, on reaching there and seeing the wild and almost impregnable character of the place, and that it was exceedingly hard to attack, did not believe he ought to try it, or work hard for no result, or make his army struggle in vain and wear itself out by encamping around it and besieging it for a long time, and waste human lives and money in vain. He thought of another possibility of mastering the town and the region without such pains and dangers.

§ 77. For this purpose he thought he had better built a fortress with a strong wall, in the midst of the district, and leave a considerable army there which should constantly ravage and plunder, and never allow the Illyrians to leave their city or come down from the mountains during the winter to till the land or to pasture or care for their flocks, or do anything else. Thus, as they would be continuously so confined and undergoing hardships, they would some day be compelled to submit to the Sultan.

Walling in of a new fortress among the Illyrians by the Sultan

§ 78. So he went through the region looking for a suitable position to fortify. He found traces and foundations of an ancient city in a favorable position, and clearly most desirable and well located in ancient times. This he decided

---

[35] George Castriota, Scanderbeg.

to fortify. He began work at the commencement of summer, with a large force and with energy and considerable expense, through his zeal and by royal oversight—for he was himself present everywhere in the work, directing everything and encouraging all the men, some by kind words, others by gifts of money, and so making them more zealous for the work. He built the fortress, a worthy and admirable piece of work. He then peopled it well, collecting very many colonists from the countryside and from the surrounding towns and cities.

§ 79. He also brought into it a great abundance of the necessities, of suitable food and of things for their service, and every other suitable and necessary thing in great abundance. He also brought in many weapons and stone-hurling cannon and crossbows and immense quantities of other materials and war supplies.

§ 80. And he fitted it out well in every particular, and made it an inhabited town, just as it had been many years before, abounding in every needful and desirable thing. He left in the fortress a considerable garrison, four hundred men from his own bodyguard, of the best fighters and the most healthy men.

§ 81. He appointed as governor of the region and commander of this large force, one of the best men of his suite, a good strategist, who was to overrun and ravage all the territory of the Illyrians systematically and unceasingly, and to besiege the town of Kroues.

§ 82. Having done this, the Sultan returned in the fall to Byzantium, taking along a very large number of slaves and animals both for himself and for distribution to the army. So closed the year 6974 in all, which was the sixteenth of the reign of the Sultan [A.D. 1466].

How the Venetians made an incursion against Old Patras

§ 63. At the very beginning of that same autumn the Venetians made an expedition against Old Patras with forty ships and 2,000 heavy infantry. They landed and besieged the city, blockading it with their army and setting up stone-throwing cannon against it. They had as allies some of the Peloponnesians who had recently revolted against the Sultan and who now joined them. And they besieged it many days, surrounding it and smashing the wall by their cannon.

How Omer attacked the Venetians, set an ambush against them, defeated them, and drove them as far as the sea, killing many and capturing many alive

§ 84. But Omer, governor-general of the Peloponnesus, with a small army, observed them from afar, setting ambushes and waiting for a favorable moment to deliver an unexpected attack. He also had some spies posted on Ox Mountain, watching everything that went on in the camp and informing him of it. So he waited for the right moment, and suddenly attacked, throwing them into confusion by the audacity of his onslaught. He turned and pursued them as far as the sea, unmercifully killing and capturing them clear to the ships and the sea itself, while they fled in disorder without any discipline. He had crushed their undertaking at the beginning.

§ 85. There perished, it was reported, about six hundred, and a little more than a hundred were captured alive. But quite a few others were drowned for, pursued by the heavy infantry and attacked on all sides, they rushed into the sea with their arms, in an attempt to swim to the ships, but being weighted down by their arms, they were pulled under.

§ 86. Omer stripped the dead and sacked the camp, securing much money for himself and his army, besides arms and equipment and all sorts of supplies. Then he put the city in good condition with the means at his command, and returned to Corinth with the captives and the booty.

§ 87. After that, with his booty and his prisoners, he went to Byzantium to the Sultan, who received him cordially and gave him rich rewards, and honored him fittingly. All the men captives he killed.

A Strange Portent

§ 88. During those same days, a wonderful light was seen in the sky, a remarkable and absolutely new sight. About the first hour of the night, which was a moonless night, there suddenly shone from the north, from the polar regions, a great fiery light, as if it came from some star. It shone all around, and lit things up like the sun. Then, spreading on from there, it went as if toward the south, in an oblique direction, like a burning pillar, remaining entire, and seemingly undiminished, but rather growing brighter and spreading. Then, stopping its progress, it kept on shining for the space of a whole hour. After that, splitting into parts and decreasing somewhat, it disappeared. Thus this portent appeared in the sky. I know not whether it was a comet, or a star, or a meteor, or some other burning object, but it certainly meant a calamity and a disaster and a very great destruction of men. And this followed in a short time, as will be clear from what follows.

§ 89. The Sultan spent the winter in Byzantium, resting from his lengthy toils, and setting things in order in the City as he saw best for the future, and erecting the mosque for himself which demanded all his care. He urged on the workmen, and ordered the architects and experts that all should be done grandly and magnificently. He himself did not spare any cost or expenditure to this end, nor show any lack of zeal. Indeed, everything possible was done for its beauty and symmetry, its surroundings, embellishment, and grandeur.

§ 90. That same winter there arrived an embassy from the Venetians, asking for a settlement of their differences, and that a treaty be made on terms of absolute equality, each party to retain what it possessed. But the Sultan would not agree to a treaty on these terms, but sent them away, saying: "Go away and prepare better terms, if you want to enjoy peace and make a treaty with me." For he demanded from them the islands of Imbros and Lemnos which they had captured, and also demanded that they pay an annual tribute.

§ 91. With things in this shape, the Sultan was informed

that Alexander, Prince of the Illyrians, had asked and secured an alliance with the Paeonians [Hungarians], that he
had roused his compatriots and secretly laid an ambush, and
that wholly without the knowledge of the Sultan's governor,
Balaban by name (whom the Sultan had left to blockade
and besiege the town of Kroues), he had astounded him by
the suddenness of his attack and had put him to flight, and
then killed many of his troops, including that Governor himself. But Balaban had put up a stiff fight.

§ 92. The Sultan heard that now Alexander had brought
into the city huge quantities of wheat, and of arms, and of
all sorts of other necessities, and that he had placed there
a stronger garrison, as was necessary for a longer siege.
It was also reported that he had gone out and taken possession of the whole region outside, and that the new fortress
was besieged, with the soldiers inside.

Second expedition of the Sultan against the Illyrians

§ 93. On hearing this news, the Sultan was very angry.
He paid no attention to anything else, but raised a very large
army of horse and foot and, after making thorough preparations—for it was already near the end of winter—as soon as
spring set in, he marched against him. On arriving in the
country of the Illyrians, he ravaged the whole of it rapidly,
and subdued its revolted people, killing many of them. He
destroyed and plundered whatever he could get hold of,
burning, devastating, ruining, and annihilating.

§ 94. He also pursued their prince, Alexander, who took
refuge in the inaccessible fortresses of the mountains, in his
customary retreats and abodes in the hills, not even daring to
behold the army, as if it were a Gorgon.

§ 95. The Sultan gave his soldiers permission to plunder
and to slaughter all the prisoners, and he sent up into the
mountains the largest and most warlike part of the army,
under Mahmud. He himself, with the rest of the army, went
on ravaging the remainder of the country, proceeding by
stages and encamping at times.

How the soldiers searched out every cranny of the mountains, and secured much booty

§ 96. And the soldiers, heavy infantry and bowmen and slingers and spearmen, on getting the signal from the Sultan, immediately charged, climbing up the highest and most rugged and inaccessible peaks of the mountains, like birds, with their weapons. They overran all parts as easily as horsemen on a plain, encountering no opposition. They searched carefully everywhere, even more so than Datis is said to have searched the region of Eretria, mountains, ravines, crevasses, precipices, caves, valleys, defiles, dens, and all holes in the ground—nothing of the kind remained hidden or escaped them, even in the most inaccessible or distant or wild or impassable sections. Not only did they capture every fortress and all who had fled into them, but they overran every place and took it, and made slaves and destroyed, for a space of fifteen days.

§ 97. They took as booty a very large number of slaves, men, women, and children, also herds of all kinds and all sorts of furnishings, and they brought them down from the mountains into the camp.

§ 98. But the prince of the Illyrians, Alexander, when he learned that the mountains had been captured by the army, hastily fled, nor have I learned whither. And the Sultan, after plundering and ravaging the countryside, marched again to Kroues. On reaching there, he encamped before it, dug a trench, and completely surrounded the town with his army, placed his cannon in position, and besieged it.

Telling of the beginning of the pestilential disease, and whence it came

§ 99. During those days, in the middle of the summer, a contagious disease struck the whole region of Thrace and Macedonia, beginning from Thessaly and its adjacent regions. I do not know how it first got to Thrace, but it spread and contaminated all the cities and districts in the interior and the coasts. Crossing also into Asia, it attacked and devastated

219

the shores of the Hellespont and the Propontis [Marmara], and it went up into the interior, to the Brousa [Bursa] region and all around there, and as far as Galatia, and it even wasted and killed people in Galatia itself.

Showing the great and terrible suffering

§ 100. It was also introduced into the great City of Constantinople, and I hardly need to say what incredible suffering it wrought there, utterly unheard-of and unbearable. More than six hundred deaths a day occurred, a multitude greater than men could bury, for there were not men enough. For some, fearing the plague, fled and never came back, not even to care for their nearest relatives, but even turned away from them, although they often appealed to them with pitiful lamentation, yet they abandoned the sick uncared-for and the dead unburied.

§ 101. Others were themselves stricken with the plague, and having a hard struggle with death, and could not help themselves. There were also some who shut themselves up in their rooms and would allow no one to come near them. Many of these died, and remained unburied for two or three days, often with nobody knowing of them. There were often two or three dead, or even more, buried in a single coffin, the only one available. And the one who today buried another, would himself be buried the next day by someone else.

§ 102. There were not enough presbyters, or acolytes, or priests for the funerals and burials or the funeral chants and prayers, nor could the dead be properly interred, for the workers gave out in the process. They had to go through the long summer days without eating or drinking, and they simply could not stand it.

§ 103. People died, some on the third day, some on the fourth, and some even on the seventh. And the terrible fact was that each day the disease grew worse, spreading among all ages, and being increasingly widespread. The City was emptied of its inhabitants, both citizens and foreigners. It had the appearance of a town devoid of all human beings, some of them dead or dying of the disease, others, as I have said, leaving their homes and fleeing, while still others shut themselves into their homes as if condemned to die. And there was great hopelessness and unbearable grief, wailing and lamentation everywhere. Despair and hopelessness dominated the spirits of all. Belief in Providence vanished altogether. People thought they must simply bear whatever happened, as though no one were presiding over events. So did the mystery of the disease perplex everyone.

As to the nature of the disease

§ 104. I shall here describe the nature of the disease. At first the malady would gain lodgement somehow in the groins, and the symptoms would appear there, more or less strong. Then it vigorously attacked the head, bringing on a high fever there, and swellings near the convolutions and membranes of the brain, and inflammation and reddening of the face. As a result of this, in some it brought unconsciousness and deep sleep and diarrhea, while in others on the contrary it brought on delirium and madness and sleeplessness.

§ 105. Then the whole pain and terrible condition would go to the heart, with a burning fever, inflaming and burning up the inner parts, and bringing on most fearful swellings, and contamination of all the blood, and its ruin. And in consequence of this, severe pains and terrible aches, and the cries of the dying, continuous sharp convulsions, hard breathing, bad odors, fearful terror, chills, insensibility of the extremities, and finally death. Such was the nature of the disease, as it appeared to me, leaving out many of the symptoms.

§ 106. The Sultan laid siege to Kroues, but not for many days, because he realized that it would be impossible to take it by assault or by force of arms, because the city was very strongly fortified and impregnable on all sides. Nor could he succeed by persuasion. So he knew he must leave a large army there with a general, to carry on a long siege, while he himself returned to Byzantium, and that he must not force himself and his army to vain attempts and struggles, when it was possible to overcome the city by starvation and by a long siege.

§ 107. So then, being of this opinion, he left a general there with a fairly large army of both seasoned and raw troops, so as to besiege the city and hold the entire region. Then he distributed all the plunder and the slaves to the entire army, and disbanded the troops and left with the royal court for Byzantium.

§ 108. But since he learned on the way that the whole region of Thrace and Macedonia and the cities in it through which he had planned to travel were in the grip of the plague and were badly devastated, and that even the great City itself was completely under the terror and destruction of it, he suddenly changed his mind, and went to the region of the Haemon and upper Moesia, for he found out that this region and all the region beyond the Haemon was free of the plague.

§ 109. As he found that the country around Nikopolis and Vidin was healthful and had a good climate, he spent the entire autumn there. But after a short time he learned that the disease was diminishing and that the City was free of it, for he had frequent couriers, nearly every day, traveling by swift relays, and reporting on conditions in the City. So at the beginning of winter he went to Byzantium. So closed the 6975th year in all [A.D. 1467], which was the seventeenth year of the reign of the Sultan.

CPSIA information can be obtained at www.ICGtesting.com
Printed in the USA
BVOW08*2214231115

428283BV00003B/4/P